To: Father Richard S. Bradford

Franklin B. Evans

600 Days in Kunming China, 1944-45

By

Tec 4 Franklin B. Evans

authorHOUSE™

1663 LIBERTY DRIVE, SUITE 200
BLOOMINGTON, INDIANA 47403
(800) 839-8640
WWW.AUTHORHOUSE.COM

This book is a work of non-fiction. Unless otherwise noted, the author and the publisher make no explicit guarantees as to the accuracy of the information contained in this book and in some cases, names of people and places have been altered to protect their privacy.

© 2005 Franklin B. Evans. All Rights Reserved.

No part of this book may be reproduced, stored in a retrieval system, or transmitted by any means without the written permission of the author.

First published by AuthorHouse 03/09/05

ISBN: 1-4208-2117-2 (sc)

Printed in the United States of America
Bloomington, Indiana

This book is printed on acid-free paper.

TABLE OF CONTENTS

PREFACE ix

GOING TO WAR xi

1. JOINING THE SERVICE - 1942 xii

2. INDUCTION TO THE ARMY 2

3. BASIC TRAINING 3

4. FURLOUGH 10

5. GOING OVERSEAS 11

6. 58 DAYS AT SEA 13

7. INDIA - 1944 21

8. TRANSPORT TO CHINA 33

9. A GREAT FLIGHT 43

10. CHINA – FIRST OF 600 DAYS 45

11. KUNMING – MY JOB 47

12. THE HUMP 54

13. DAY BY DAY AT AIR FREIGHT 62

14. PILOTS 83

15. KUNMING LIFE 87

16. ROTATION 99

17. COCA COLA'S FAILURE TO LIVE UP TO PROMISES MADE TO PRESIDENT ROOSEVELT OR WHY COCA COLA FAILED IN CHINA IN WWII 103

18. OTHER WAR MEMORIES 115

19. GOING HOME!	120
20. BACK IN THE U.S.A.	124
21. FINAL 'ARMY' THOUGHTS	128
22. EPILOGUE	131
23. SOURCE MATERIAL	133
24. PHOTOS	137

PREFACE

This is being recorded fifty-seven years after I got out of the United States Army. It is based upon the memory of an eighty-year old man, although my memory is in better shape than a lot of the rest of my body. Besides my own memories of World War II, I have help, as my father saved my wartime letters, and I have nine V-mails (Victory-mails) and twenty-three other letters written from overseas. Also, in January 1946 I went to St. Petersburg, Florida, to visit my maternal grandfather, with whom I had lived for many years of my life. He was interested in hearing some of my World War II stories, and said they should be saved for my great-great-great grandchildren. Part of his interest was because I was the first member of the family (which had ancestors back to the early seventeenth century in New England) that had ever served in the Army overseas. Earlier relatives had served in the Revolutionary War, at least one in the Civil War, and my father in World War I. Also, John Hancock and John Brown of Harpers Ferry were uncles. So each day after I told him my stories, my grandfather typed them up. Although he was partially blind by then, and over 90 years old, he wrote nine pages of notes for me.

My letters contain few factual details about the war, as they were written overseas and were subject to censorship. One couldn't write down the words like "in the air raid" or many things that one did. So the letters are somewhat limited but they do help. Also, in 1954 I wrote five pages of notes about a particular conflict I had with the Coca-Cola Company. It will be included under that title later on in these notes. Also included are many personal views, things that I did and that happened to me that may some day be of interest to someone else. Remember that most opinions are idiosyncratic—peculiar to the individual.

These notes are being taped and transcribed at the requests of my children, who, over the years, have heard most of what follows. They were influenced by Tom Brokaw's two books about <u>The Greatest Generation</u>. Brokaw, I'm sure, caused a lot of work for several thousand WWII veterans.

> (Aside: One day in the summer of 2000 in a large grocery store in Michigan, I was approached by a clean-cut young man about 20-25 years old. He asked me if I had been in WWII and said he had been reading Brokaw's <u>Greatest Generation</u>. I told him that I had been in the Army and in China. He then insisted on shaking my hand and in a loud voice, thanked me and our greatest generation. I was embarrassed. None of the academic articles I had published years ago ever caused a reaction like that.

Recording ten hours of memories has not been an easy task. It brought back a lot of things, some good and some I wish I had forgotten. I've laughed at myself a few times and cried for the starving Indian and Chinese children I saw. I thank my children and grandchildren for their support and tolerance. <u>Please remember that these memories are from tape transcriptions— not much edited</u>. I dedicate these notes to my wife, Bobbie, who died in 1997. After seven days of married life (1943) she then waited for over two years for me to return.

I also wish to thank Trisha Johnson who has assiduously and prudently transcribed all my tapes.

GOING TO WAR

The summer of 1941, at the end of my sophomore year at the University of Chicago, at the age of nineteen, I managed to travel in the Pacific. I went to Hawaii, Samoa, Fiji and both islands of New Zealand and had a great time. The reason for the trip in the Pacific was that I couldn't make the usual family tour of Europe as Europe was already at war. On the way back from my trip, I stopped in Hawaii for five weeks, most of August and the first part of September. At that time, everyone I talked to in Honolulu, was expecting war with Japan. Newspapers were full of stories about how the Japanese were reacting to the U.S. embargo on shipping of steel for war materials, etc. The newspapers were printing stories, for example, of how Japanese tuna fishing boats sailing from Honolulu (where there was a cannery) were restricted to not more than 600 miles from Hawaii and were given only enough diesel fuel to go that far. Their fear was that they would refuel Japanese submarines that might be around. Also, there were reports, although not necessarily true, of sightings of Japanese submarines within a few hundred miles of Hawaii. The Navy was patrolling the skies north of Hawaii for three to four hundred miles with PBY flying boats. The typical reaction to seeing one flying over Diamond Head or Waikiki when I was sitting on the beach or drinking beer at the Waikikian Bar, a sailor next to you would look up and say something like "Well, that's a PBY, they're ours but the next one might be Japanese". The point is that the people in Hawaii were expecting the conflict with the Japanese, which happened, of course, on December 7, 1941. I told these stories to anybody who would listen to me when I came back, but nobody paid any attention to them.

1. JOINING THE SERVICE - 1942

In 1942, I was twenty years old and a junior at the University of Chicago, most of my peers and I were looking for the best service to join. We were checking the opportunities of the recruitment being done on campus. Most of the programs had three things in common. First, you were supposed to be allowed to finish your college to get your degree before called to duty. Second, you were supposed to pick three and get a choice of branches of the service you were in and what you did. Third, you would be given a chance of OCS training. As the recruiters came by, I decided that I wanted to be in the Air Corps, the most glamorous and it's what my father had been in World War I. It seemed like a great thing and I liked airplanes a lot. I'd flown but I had never learned how to do it. I started out with the Army Air Corps (which was part of the Army at that time) and found that I didn't qualify because of my eyes. The Air Corps wanted everybody to be 20-20 or correct up to 20-20 in both eyes. My left eye corrects to only about 20-200 and the right eye was 20-40, so there went the Army Air Corps. The next that came along and I tried for was the Naval Air Corps, with the same results. Then I finally tried the Marine Air Corps. The first thing they did was to test my eyes again. Then they pointed to the door. I looked over some other opportunities but then the Army came along with a program that offered essentially the same thing that as previous ones, I signed up with the United States Army (regular Army). One of the first priorities was not to be a draftee, so I signed up on August 18, 1942. The status was inactive service at that time. My serial number was 16081054, which showed I'd enlisted as opposed to being drafted—all draftees' serial numbers started with '3'. Sometimes this was an advantage, other times the opposite. I was told to report to Fort Custer in Battle Creek, Michigan for induction on April 29, 1943 into our regular Army.

There is one other notable thing that I have any notes on from 1942 (and this is something that I did not learn about until several years later when I went back to the University of Chicago for my second and third degrees). The west stands of Stag Field contained several squash courts that the government had taken over. Stag Field was not being used any more for football had been dropped the end of 1939. We knew at the time that some kinds of experiments were going on there. This was when "man's first self-sustaining nuclear reaction took place on December 2, 1942." Among the people who had made the world's first nuclear self-sustaining atomic reaction were Fermi and Szilard and several others, probably a total of a dozen people in their scientific group. Nobody on campus knew what they were working on. After World War II I heard that on the date when the first self-sustaining reaction happened, the scientists who developed the atomic pile, were overjoyed to see that it was actually working. They were so happy with it they were congratulating each other and someone brought out a bottle of wine and they were all having a drink and toasting each other with their success. After a time someone said "Shouldn't we put the graphite rods back into the pile? It's getting pretty hot." If the reaction had not been stopped, all of the University of Chicago and probably half of the south side of the city with it would have gone up in the world's first atomic explosion and I would have been one of them because I was on campus that day. That's what I remember thinking.

1943

2. INDUCTION TO THE ARMY

On April 29, 1943, I reported to the Army, at Fort Custer, Michigan, along with what seemed like a thousand others, mostly draftees. Induction consisted of things which were dear to the Army. First you got your uniforms and then received shots and another physical exam. We got shots for everything that anybody had ever thought of, and took some tests. One test considered most important was an Army IQ test (AGCT). The test had an average score of 100; officers were supposed to have a score of 110 or more. I scored 144 so I wasn't too far from the top. I knew a few people in the same range as me. I think the maximum score was 155 (I can best describe it now as a forerunner of an SAT test that everybody takes to see which college will accept them).

I stayed at Fort Custer for about a week and learned that the Army was mostly "hurry up and wait." I can't say that I enjoyed it there, but we certainly got enough shots. At the end of the week, about when I was wondering when they were going to come ask me which branch I wanted to serve in, the bulletin board posted the assignments and shipping orders for the next day or two. They were simply by alphabet; all those unlucky people whose names started with A-B-C, went to the infantry in Fort Benning, Georgia. Those whose names started with E-F-G-H-I were to report to Fort Sill, Oklahoma.

3. BASIC TRAINING

The first thing at Fort Sill was to mark everything you owned – clothing, books, etc., with your serial number, in my case, 16081054. I was assigned to Battery E, 32nd Battalion, 8th Regiment Field Artillery, Field Artillery Replacement Training Center. The original schedule was for 13 weeks of training in instrument and survey. The training part was learning how to direct howitzer fire. The classes were not difficult; I would say about a sophomore in high school level of algebra.

A typical day at Fort Sill was:

Mornings – Reveille at 6:00 a.m.

Breakfast, Calisthenics, Close-order drill (marching)

Classes on surveying and map reading

Afternoons –

Lunch, weapon study, propaganda movies (to hate all Germans and Japanese) and sex horror films (the dangers of VD)

Field exercises and 5-10 mile hikes

Dinner – 6:00 p.m.

Taps – 10:00 p.m.

The difficult part for me, a person who believed one had to drive a car if you wanted to go over a block, was the physical side of it. The first three or four weeks, I thought I was going to drop dead from the physical exertion I was not used to.

By the time I finished the first 13 weeks in Fort Sill, I was in the best physical condition of my life. I had lost a lot of fat and maybe 5-10 pounds, but I enjoyed feeling that way. I liked the ten mile marches and found there is such a thing as second wind when hiking--I actually wished we had more of them. I also found that after the first few days when I thought calisthenics would kill me, that they were the greatest. We had a half hour of them first thing every morning--I really wished they had gone on for an hour because it was so much fun to jump up in the air and clap hands.

Our battery (or company) in the army was about 60 people, most of whom were college students from Colorado, who had one advantage. They had all been enrolled in ROTC at college and were taken en masse to join this company in the field artillery. Incidentally, before leaving Chicago, I had enough courses for my degree. My Chicago degree was sent to me in the mail.

The artillery instructors who taught the courses were not very bright, but they were both from Chicago so we had some things to talk about. The work was interesting in general.

There were only a couple of people from Fort Custer that ended up in the same platoon I was in, but I made quite a few new friends. The one that I remember best was an Indian from New Mexico, who had served a hitch in the Army before and then had reenlisted. He helped me a great deal, teaching me about the Army and how to get along in the Army way of doing things and to some extent, the Army way of avoiding things. Particularly, the sacred Army practice of "scrounging" when you need something, there were ways of "scrounging" it out without having to try to go through proper channels and paperwork and approvals. He had been a champion boxer when he was in the Army the first time, and they kept trying to get him to join the boxing cadre at Fort Sill, but he wouldn't.

He helped me in two more ways. One was to quit walking around slightly slouched over and not standing up straight. Every time he passed me, he hit me with his fist in the middle of my back and it was a good hard hit too. I had black and blue marks for a while and I very quickly learned to stand up straight and not to walk around with my hands in my pockets. After being hit a few dozen times in the middle of the back, one learns. Also, he taught me to stand on my head as a manner of relaxation, which I didn't believe until I did it. After you've done it a few times, you find that it's really pretty easy to stand on your head and it does become relaxing. I could stand on my head for an hour if I wanted to, and did so a couple of times just to see how far I could go. It was something that stayed with me too. I used to occasionally, as late as the 1970's, amuse friends and my children, by standing on my head after dinner or after one too many drinks when we were in Hawaii, at a party, everyone could find me standing on my head in the middle of the living room. Those were the important things I learned in Fort Sill except that the Army was certainly a different kind of life.

(Here are a couple of other Oklahoma notes that I made.) One was that after about four or five weeks at Fort Sill, everybody in the Company that had a score on the Army GCT (General Classification Test) over 110 was asked to pick three branches of OCS that you would like to go to, with a strong hint being for everybody being smart to mark down field artillery. So, I did, I put field artillery, transportation (the army had more ships than the Navy actually), and my third choice was quarter master. I figured my business education would help. Along with all of the college people (except one who couldn't score 110, but had a lot of military experience from ROTC at Texas A & M) filled out these forms and then a week later we were told that there were no openings anywhere. That took care of that.

Among the training things that I recall was having to go through a bunch of small rooms with different kinds of gas, in a weak form of course, but you were to learn to recognize what fosagene gas and mustard gas smell like. The final room was tear gas so everybody came out of this one crying--it looked like a funeral seeing a whole bunch of soldiers, 45 to 50 of them, all crying like babies.

Another test was the infiltration course everyone had to go through. You had to crawl on your stomach about 60 yards, (it seemed like 60 miles at the time) and you had to wiggle your way under barbed wire, small fenced off areas next to you were full of quarter dynamite sticks exploding and there was live machine gun fire 16" off the ground. You had to stay under it if you didn't want to get shot and you had to do it as fast as you could. I got through in the first ten out of my whole company, so I was in good shape. At the end of the course, medics were there with iodine for all your scratches from the barbed wire. I had at least 100 of them and it ruined my uniform, which would catch in the barbed wire but you had to keep going. If you didn't go fast enough, one of the training cadre would throw a quarter stick of dynamite, a lit fuse like a cherry bomb, behind you. That encouraged you to get under the barbed wire that was staked to the ground quite tightly.

We also had a fair amount of small arms training, which was easy enough for me because I was used to firearms. Most of the training was with a 1906 Springfield bolt action, 30 caliber Army rifle, although the semi-automatic Garand was the one being used for combat. The training was all with a 30.06 cartridge.

Near Fort Sill was Lawton, Oklahoma, and like many small towns next to a large Army base, the natives quickly learn that they don't like the Army, and that their purpose in life in a small town is to separate the Army personnel, (and I think there were about 80,000 to 90,000 people at Fort Sill at the time), from whatever money they had. So, I didn't spend much time in Lawton, although I did find one place where you could get a fairly decent sandwich for 50 cents.

I did manage a two-day visit to Oklahoma City, which was 75 to 80 miles away. It was fun to get away and stay in a hotel. Oklahoma was a dry state then, and every cab driver was a bootlegger. For three or four dollars, would quickly produce a pint of whiskey for you. I had my fill of that. Beer was readily available all over Oklahoma City and you could eat prairie oysters and drink 3.2 beer, and the effects weren't too bad. Like a lot of people, we gobbled up prairie oysters like mad because they were free. Then, we found out what they were and suddenly everybody stopped eating them. (That's enough of that story.)

Training in Fort Sill was supposed to be 13 weeks long and the last 10 days of this were to be spent in the field, where we pitched our pup tents, and looked out for the snakes, as that part of Oklahoma was full of rattlesnakes. (As a side note, I doubt if we ever went on a march in rocky terrain of Fort Sill, where we didn't spot one or more rattlesnakes, which usually met their demise as soldiers threw rocks as big as 20 pounds at the snakes until they disappeared from life). This was my first experience at real camping out, so it was really quite interesting and fun. Even though we were sleeping in a tent on the hard ground, the only real complaint I had about Oklahoma was the heat. It was late June and early July, and it often reached 110 degrees or more. It was very hot, humid, and lots of wind. There were times when dust twirled in small tornadoes that rose about 15 feet.

They were called "dustdevils" and as they swirled all around, they covered you with dust. If you were lucky, a thunderstorm would come through, and there were plenty of them too. Then you were not only covered with dust, but it was dust that had turned into mud from the thunderstorms. Fort Sill was not a pleasant place, weather-wise in the summer.

Just about the time we finished our 13 weeks of basic training in Fort Sill, the Army decided that they didn't really need so many replacements and although people were still being drafted, basic training was extended for another month, to a total of 17 weeks. This was all right, except that they had no plans of what people were to do during the last four weeks. We spent a great deal of time walking around, taking hikes, and maybe extra time to go to the PX, but little formal training. They hadn't planned on anything past 13 weeks and the military was not very good at improvising.

At the same time the Army opened up a new program, ASTP (which stood for Army Student Training Program), that was available to anyone who had any college at all. Most of them were being sent to the University of Texas to study things like the weather or take classes in the Japanese language. In the ten days while GIs were signing up for ASTP, we lost most of the other college people in the platoon. I was the only one who refused to sign. I simply told the recruiting people for ASTP, that I had finished 16 years of schooling, I had my college degree, and I was not going back to school. I had not joined the Army to go to school again; I had had enough of that and I wanted to go overseas. At the time, I was so fed up with Oklahoma and Fort Sill that I wrote my father and told him that I was volunteering to go to New Guinea immediately to get out of Oklahoma.

The Army obliged in its own way, and after the 17th week, I was given a 10-day furlough which was a highly important part of my life.

4. FURLOUGH

When the furlough came along, about mid-September, I went to Chicago by train, courtesy of the Army, or at least they paid for it. I had telephoned and made arrangements the previous week with Barbara, and we got married September 16, 1943. We were married in her house. Her mother got us a cake and an Episcopal minister was there. We said our vows. Bobbie's mother, my father, brother, and his wife and a couple of neighbors were all that were present at the wedding. I knew some of the people, including Barbara's mother, didn't approve of this little girl, who was three years younger than me, marrying a soldier. It took them quite a few years to decide that I was all right. Bobbie and I had seven days together before I had to leave to go overseas. We spent four of those days taking a trip in one of my father's company automobiles. We went to Macatawa, Michigan, and then up to look at the home in Leland, Michigan, that my father had purchased that summer.

Anyway, it was a good move for me and Bobbie, and it lasted as long as she lived (to 1997). We had almost 54 years of married life before she passed on. (Here it is 6 years later, and I am still going on.)

5. GOING OVERSEAS

After my ten-day furlough, marriage and wonderful time with Bobbie, I had to report to Fort Ord, California, where GIs were gathered to be shipped overseas. I was in Fort Ord for the good part of October and the first week of November 1943.

Fort Ord was an interesting experience, but there were only a few things for us to do, one of which was to go to the rifle ranges and shoot the Garand rifle. This not too fun because the Garand weighed about nine pounds and kicked like a Tennessee mule. After shooting maybe a 100 rounds, one's shoulder was black and blue. Nonetheless, having had experience with guns before the Army, I did qualify and my discharge shows MM Rifle, which is marksman. I guess if I wanted, I could add a marksman medal to my other paraphernalia from the Army.

We also had to go through another infiltration course like the one at Fort Sill, but the one at Fort Ord, California was a lot easier than the one in Oklahoma, because it was in sandy country, and you could wiggle through the sand on your stomach and elbows a lot easier than in Oklahoma dirt.

An experience at Fort Ord that wasn't difficult were hikes through the sand dunes and hills around Fort Ord, probably about 10 miles each. One of them was an overnighter with full packs and half-tents. We had to pitch the tents around midnight and a level spot with trees and bushes was picked. The weather wasn't too bad, although it was chilly at night at Fort Ord in September and October. Anyhow, we camped there and returned the next day. About two days later, of the 70 in the platoon, at least three-fourths came down with the worst cases of poison oak that you ever saw. We had stayed in poison oak country and everybody slept in it. Some people had forgotten to bring toilet paper and were using poison oak leaves for that purpose. Pretty soon, the whole platoon and the one next to it, who had been on the same hike with us, were the funniest looking bunch you ever saw. Almost everyone was covered in calamine lotion, except for the few, including me, who were lucky and didn't get into the poison oak. I never saw so many people covered in calamine lotion, scratching, and complaining. Poison oak is considered even worse than poison ivy.

Fort Ord is on Monterey Bay and when one had the time, he could walk down to the beach, especially on a pleasant fall day. The bay was full of fishing boats and large groups of seals swimming along the shore, anywhere from six to twenty in groups, about every five minutes, making lots of noise and having fun.

Fort Ord is near Monterrey, California, which in those days, was an interesting fishing village. It had one hotel and 8-10 small canneries. On the north end of the bay, the fisherman would catch sardines, come back and dump them at the canneries on the waterfront. In no time, they were in the cans. (I have heard that about 20 years ago, Monterrey Bay was fished out and there hasn't been a sardine there for many years now.

I had a couple of chances to drive around the bay down past Carmel, which was a beautiful bay. I'm not sure, but there was probably a golf course there then, but I was not able to play golf in Carmel.

Early November, I was sent to Riverside, California, which was in the desert southeast of Los Angeles. It was a POE (Port of Embarkation). My orders called for shipment to China – Z-Forces. I then knew where I was going but I couldn't tell anybody.

6. 58 DAYS AT SEA

We were shipped out on Thanksgiving Day, 1943. I and the others on the order were loaded on a truck and taken to the waterfront at Wilmington.

We were loaded onto a brand new liberty ship, which was loaded and ready to sail; the deck cargo of P-40 fighter planes were chained and welded down to the hatches. We asked about our accommodations and were pointed to a wooden box about 15 feet long and maybe 7 feet wide, with a door and window on each end. Inside were bunks, three high for a dozen. There were eleven of us assigned to this wooden box, located on the life boat deck, port side.

There was a similar wooden box on the other side, which we learned later contained half a dozen Chinese pilots who had been trained in Texas. We never saw them; they just never came out day or night and they lived in their wooden box until they got off in India. At one time, I tried to get some of my compatriots in our wooden box to go and raid the other just to make sure the Chinese weren't chained in. Of course, we never did. The Liberty ship was new, on its maiden voyage, 441'6" long, and 57 feet wide. They were old fashioned in many ways, had five cargo holds and an oil fed boiler for the three cylinder steam engine.

There were six anti-aircraft 20 mm machine gun tubs, three per side and on the aft deck over the rudder, there was another cabin, which had a single 3-inch 50 gun (shell 3" diameter, 50" long) on it. The U.S. Navy Armed Guard of 20 lived in the aft cabin, only one of whom had been on a ship before. They had no more idea of what was going on or where we were going than anybody else. The merchant marine crew (non-military) of 18, were in the center of the ship. The old-timers were obviously very good sailors, but some of the crew were young men that signed on to get out of jail. They weren't particularly desirable types.

On the third day out, the captain of the liberty ship announced that there would be no ship drills or similar foolishness on this trip. We were going alone as an armed liberty ship, testing a new route to India. Of the five cargo holds on the ship, four were labeled in red, which means highly explosive. The first three contained bombs, some of which were gas. The fourth hold on the liberty ship contained aviation gas, 100 octane in 55 gallon drums, not the safest way to carry it. The fifth hold contained small arms and ammunition of assorted kinds and the ship's food, etc.

We sailed directly south, from California at a steady speed of 11 knots. We continued sailing south-southwest for almost a week. We saw no other ships or planes, only some islands with greenery on them, maybe 30 miles away. I was never close enough to tell what they were, probably part of the Society Islands, but we sure didn't see any Tahaitian girls.

After sailing for two weeks or so, we were getting into cold weather - beyond a south latitude of 50 degrees, then we turned in a westerly direction. About a week or so later, according to the crew, we passed a small island where the New Zealanders had a weather station which had been attacked by the crew of a Nazi submarine in 1940 or 1941, (I forget which date). The New Zealanders' weather crew were all shot on the spot. We sailed south of New Zealand's South Island.

The liberty ship continued to the west until we came in sight of a very large island, which turned out to be Tasmania, part of

Australia, about 500 miles south of Sidney. We then turned into a large bay, at the end is the Port of Hobart, the main and only large town in Tasmania. The day we arrived there was the 24th of December 1943. As soon as the ship was tied up at the dock, we started taking on oil, fuel that was needed for the rest of the trip. Those of us who were not tied to jobs on the ship, immediately went ashore and looked for ways to do something. A friend of mine and I ended up in a bar on the main street of Hobart where we consumed as much whisky (scotch) as we could drink. The rest of the money we had, we invested in bottles of scotch to take back to the ship, when we finally ran out of the energy to drink anymore. As it turned out, it didn't do us much good to take any back to the ship. By the time we got back, we were pretty well floating in scotch and immediately passed out. When we woke up, all the scotch we had bought had been taken by the crew, so we never did get to drink the six or seven bottles we brought back from the bar. Hobart, though, was an interesting town. People were very nice and friendly. The town was full of old cars, 1930's; they looked like they were brand new, probably because there wasn't very far on the Island of Tasmania to drive.

We set sail early the next morning, which was Christmas Day. We had been 30 days from Wilmington, California to Hobart. You can't go much slower than that.

A few more remarks about the liberty ship have occurred to me that I probably passed over before. One, the Liberty ship that I sailed on, (whose name I cannot recall at the moment), was brand new; the Naval Armed Guard of 20 men, were quite proud of the fact that they were the first armed guard crew to be on a Liberty ship, sailing alone (that is not in convoy or with any escorts of any kind) around the whole Pacific. The Navy crew, who were fairly young, aligned themselves, more or less, with us, as opposed to the merchant marine sailors who were paid as much per day as any of us made in a month.

There wasn't enough crew with the twenty of them to man the anti-aircraft 20 millimeter machine guns, and 3 inch-50 in the stern. Nine of the eleven of us signed up with the Navy to do certain jobs on the different guns. I was selected for the job of hot shell man on the 3 inch 50. I wore a heavy asbestos apron from shoulders to below the knees and gloves that went from the tops of your arms to your hands. My job was to catch the shells when they were ejected from the gun and throw them overboard. The large brass casings weighed about 15 pounds each, and when they came out, they were very <u>hot</u>. We had, besides a lot of dry-run training, at least three instances testing live ammunition. The machine guns shot at balloons inflated with gas, tossed up in the air. The 3 inch 50 had targets made of used orange crates and boxes tied together, anything left over from the galley, was tossed overboard. When they were about 800 yards astern, we shot at them. The only problem was with the 3 inch, as we never came close to any of the targets and the anti-aircraft machine gunners never hit a single balloon. I figured we weren't going to be much danger to any Japanese or German submarines that showed up. They would have had to have been as big as the Queen Mary for us to hit. Fortunately, nothing happened in that sense.

We did have two alerts, once in the Pacific and once more at the beginning of the Indian Ocean. The radio operator had picked up reports of Japanese submarines being somewhere in the area. We and the Navy Armed Guard crew went on four hour watch, four hours on and fours off, for general quarters alert. The first one lasted three days and the second one lasted four days. You found that after four days with four on and four off, all you wanted to do was sleep. The only outcome of joining the Navy for a couple of months caused our service records to show we had served with the Navy. So we, as soldiers, were also honored by the Navy and given the American Defense Medal and the ribbon that goes with it, which I still have.

One other item of some interest to somebody was that the Navy men on the ship wanted somebody to fight a three-round boxing match with one of their people. I ended up being picked (I guess because nobody else was the right weight of 135 pounds) to represent the Army. What I didn't know until much later was that the Navy candidate was a ringer in the sense that he had fought in the Catholic Youth Organization (CYO) in New York, and had some training as a boxer. Mine came mostly from time spent in physical ed at Fort Sill. Anyway, we agreed to have a three-round match of three 3-minute rounds, which was too long, but I donned the 16 ounce gloves. The first round went pretty well and I did manage to get in one haymaker and knocked the other guy down. The general opinion was that I won the first round. The second round, we just sort of chased each other around the hatch (ring) of the ship and nobody did much of anything. By the third round, those 16-ounce gloves felt like they weighed 16 tons and I wasn't doing much of anything. The sailor did nothing but pound on me for three minutes; he didn't manage to knock me down or out or anything, but the generally agreed outcome by the spectators was a draw, so we were able to hold our heads up a little bit.

The other thing that I don't think I mentioned before was that the engineering part of the Liberty Ship was interesting.

I had never seen anything like it before. The chief engineer, a merchant marine engineer for most of his life, an elderly man, let us go in several times and showed us the engines, which were large 3-cylinder steam engines, with the steam produced by oil-fired boilers. The first cylinder was about two feet in diameter and six or seven feet high. The second one was another foot wider and a couple of feet shorter, which got the steam that the first one didn't use. The third cylinder was about like a 55-gallon drum in size, three feet across and four feet high and got the remaining steam which went back into the tanks to be reheated for more steam. The boiler used a lot of oil, and the ship didn't go very fast, but it went. The moss that grew along the ship's waterline was 6 inches or more by the time we left the warm South Pacific.

We left very early in the morning on December 26, from Hobart, Tasmania, and headed south back towards Antarctica again. After maybe four or five hours sailing, we were not only out of sight of Tasmania, headed straight south, but far enough south where it was very cold, well beyond fifty degrees south. The ocean started to live up to the reputation of the frightful 50's. The roaring 40's were nothing like the frightful 50's, and we saw waves that were unbelievable. They pounded into the Liberty ship from about noon until four o'clock and the waves were large enough to lift the whole stern of the Liberty ship. The propeller would race while up in the air, as the waves came over the bow thirty feet deep, doing this for about five or six hours. The waves were as high as the bridge of the Liberty ship, which must have been about 50-60 feet above what would have been water level. We pounded into these waves, closely spaced, for hours, maybe every minute or two, until the captain got concerned about the airplanes that were chained and welded on the hatches. There was solid water coming over the decks from one end of the ship to the other. When the propeller came out of the water up into the air the whole ship shook like a leaf and as the bow then rose on the next wave water on the deck smashed into the doors (hatches) of the center "island" of the ship. The shaking of the ship loosened the doors and the ship's Bosun ran from one side of the island to the other using a large wooden mallet to beat down the latches (dogs) that held the doors closed. He had to do this for hours. Then the captain turned ship and reduced the propeller RPMs just enough to keep the ship headed into the waves. This went on all night: in the morning, we were still headed into the wind and only about 15 miles behind us was Tasmania; the storm had driven us at least 60 miles backwards. The storm was abating so the propeller RPMs were raised to 100, and we started back on our voyage to India, continuing west until I was sure we were going to run into Africa, at least Madagascar. We were so far south of the main continent of Australia that we never saw it. When we got to the longitude where India began, we made another turn to starboard and headed towards Karachi. We arrived in Karachi 28 days from Tasmania. The whole trip to India from California was 58 days on the Liberty ship.

  We did finally, in the Indian Ocean, come upon the only ship we had seen since we left California. It was a small Australian troop ship with an Australian Navy corvette escort coming towards us and zigzagging. They would go ten minutes in one direction and then change course 90 degrees. (I suppose this indicated some fear of what was out there. The liberty ship never did that, we just sailed a straight course). At one point, we were close enough to wave at them and the Aussies waved back.

On the final day we pulled into the harbor at Karachi, India. My first view was of large Arab dhow, with a lug sail that extended from the bow to top of the mast, and then 40 feet aft to the stern. The lug had to be dipped each time they changed directions. Surprisingly, they sailed quite well and almost as fast as the liberty ship. We landed at a quay on the river in Karachi, got off and were taken to an American Army camp about 20 miles away in the desert.

7. <u>INDIA - 1944</u>

Karachi was an eye-opener for someone who had never been to the Orient. To suddenly get off a ship, and see a street with camels running around, some loose, others pulling carts, people with turbans, the entire scene was something you wouldn't believe. There were a few trucks, but not many, and a fair number of British soldiers.

The camp of about 1,000 men was in the middle of a desert, and like any other desert, it got terribly hot in the daytime, perhaps 115 degrees, and this was January 1944. You quickly wanted to take a shower, and three-a-day was better than one. It was quite chilly at night though, the desert cooled off in a hurry. One of the first things I noticed, (certainly new to me) was the desert area was full of jackals, which are not quite wolves, but of that variety. They bay at the moon and bark all night, especially when the moon is full. It was a very eerie experience, and when we didn't hear them, we kind of missed the noise.

We did very little while we were in the camp outside Karachi, mostly a lot of waiting around, and I stood guard duty a couple of times. It gave the MPs a chance to relax and let somebody else guard the stockade for a night or two, which is about as dull as you can get, watching prisoners sleep. It wasn't bad duty, it was just another way of passing time. We went to Karachi several times to eat and the food was not too bad. I found that I could eat the rice with a few other tidbits. There were all different sects of Indians, and all were relatively friendly towards Americans, but they sure hated the British. Every building and wall in this part of India had two words on them "QUIT INDIA". This was the work of the Indian Nationalist Party, and it was unbelievable that they had made so many signs and such political feeling. The radio station in Karachi (being in the Muslim part of India) had daily long broadcasts by the Muslim leader, Mohammed Ali Jinah, who was Oxford educated, and spoke better English than any of my compatriots. He made sense, talking about the fact that the people themselves should rule their own country. We didn't get any contact or hear anything from Mohandus Gandhi because the British had him in jail. Jinah impressed a lot of people as there was not much else that was interesting to hear. You quickly tired of every time you turned around, you would see another sign that said "QUIT INDIA".

The only new person I met in this camp outside of Karachi, was a sergeant in the British Army, who had been in India, (at least if you believed his story) for over five years. He had all kinds of wild tales of the frontier, and he adopted the Americans, or we adopted him. He insisted that our food was delicious and much better than English Army food or even local restaurants. In the beginning, he ate with us three meals a day. He couldn't seem to get enough. Pretty soon, he moved into one of the tents that happened to be the one I was in. Then he was an around-the-clock visitor, he never did go back to the British camp. About the time I was leaving, some British MPs found him; he was AWOL from his own unit, a British camp a few miles away. He was an interesting person and certainly prepared us more for what we would see in India, such as the poverty, the people, and the British attitude towards them.

This attitude was nobody was any good who wasn't British. The Anglo-Indians were somewhat accepted; there were many hundreds of thousands of them in India, almost all with British fathers and Indian mothers. The "Anglos" ran the railroads, banks, and most of the government jobs were reserved for them.[1] The English believed that Indians were sub-human. I suspect that the Americans treated the slaves the same way during the Civil War times. The British didn't have any compassion for the Indians.

We spent almost three weeks in this camp in Karachi and then went across the country to Calcutta and on to Upper Assam, the far eastern part of India, to fly to China. So we packed our barracks bags again, the group that I had come over on the ship lost a couple of guys to the MPs. They decided they would rather stay and become MPs in Ceylon. The other nine of us from the original eleven got train tickets to Calcutta, and a little Bakshees money. Bakshees is a tip if you want to call it that. It was what every Indian said to every American. We got our tickets upgraded to first class so we rode in a very deluxe British styled carriage that had compartment doors that opened out on the platform. On the cross Indian line, it was a pretty fancy train; the gage of the train was wider than those we had in the United States. The line went north as far as Lahore, which is now the capital of Pakistan. We did not get to go through Delhi, the capital of India or Agra, where I had hoped we would go and see the Taj Majal. It was interesting countryside, and also on the train, we could buy beer. The train trip took us 3 ½ days to Calcutta. Just before we got to Calcutta, we started seeing results of famine in India. There was a very bad famine in the fall and winter in Bengal, a major province of India. Trains kept going by, with thousands of people riding the trains in every possible place. Not only in the

---

[1] I might add that I've heard that after the British left, one of the first things the Indian Government did was to get the Anglo Indians out of all the major government jobs and railroads.

cars, but boxcars filled solid with people and there might be two to three hundred people crammed on the roof of the car. There were another eight to ten on each end of the car, hanging onto the ladders that led up to the roof. People were riding on the side of the engine, next to the boiler, and a half dozen people riding in the front (cow-catcher) of the engine. These trains, who normally held a few hundred people, were suddenly loaded with a couple of thousand. They were starving people, farmers who had lost everything, going to large cities with the hopes of being fed by the government. It was a real view of poverty like one had never seen, heard, or believed could happen anywhere in the world, but here it was. We were given instructions even before we left Karachi, but also on the train that when we got to Calcutta to the Howrah railroad station in Calcutta, not to give any money to beggars. If you gave even a rupee, you would be mobbed by hundreds or more beggars, and your clothes would be torn off. We were told to debark as quickly as possible and not to give anybody anything.

About the money in India: a rupee was worth approximately 32 cents when I was there. Twelve annas to a rupee were in coin form, and they had one anna, half an anna, five annas, and so forth coins. It was a completely different system of money, and was hard to manage for people used to decimal everything. The rupee was, to the Indians, like two dollars or more to us. One could be pulled around town in a rickshaw for an hour for 8 annas. The British rode in the same kind of rickshaws, and they would give them 6 annas, where we gave them a rupee. No wonder they liked the Americans better, we couldn't understand their money, and we gave them more of it. The British also, and unfortunately, referred to all Indians as "wogs." In a typical

American or British fashion, they called people names that were a pejorative type of use. So what you got, was people calling them "wogs" and treating them as such, or worse.

One other thing I noticed that was certainly different to me from anything you see in this country was that there were little shrines all along the roads that had fires and circles of stones. There wasn't much chance to talk to Indians because of all the different languages, but fortunately, many spoke English and had been to school. The one thing that was good about English was that it tied the whole country together, where there were at least 100 different languages. The major languages were Urdu and Hindustani, but only a quarter of the people in the whole continent spoke one of those two. The others had their own languages.

We had brought our own food on the train, C-ration cans, which you learned to like when you looked at the alternatives, including monkey meat. At every station the train stopped in, the platform was full of food sellers, with trays with all kinds of food and curries and tea. The tea was drinkable, and cheap, only a couple of annas for a cup of tea. At least you knew that if the water was boiled, it was probably safe.

After we finally got to Calcutta, on the 4th day of the train across, we got some directions from other Americans who were wandering around. We found a Red Cross run dormitory, where we could stay for ten days. So, we had ten days to learn about Calcutta, which at that time was one of the three largest cities in the world, and with all the people coming from the country because they were starving, there were tremendous crowds of people everywhere. Calcutta had almost ten million at that time. The streets were full of sacred cows wandering around, and nobody would do anything except occasionally kick them and push them out of the way. Cars would bump into them gently to get moving. Cow dung was picked up, made into patties, dried, and burned as fuel for their stoves, and the smoke smelled!

Calcutta was the first place that any of us had been where we were exposed to the caste system. Caste set status and jobs and that was all one could have. You were born into a caste, and stayed there. The higher caste was mostly Brahman; the lowest were the untouchables, the ones that Gandhi had associated with to prove that the system was bad and tried to get them to change but they never did. The ones that cleaned the streets and the urinals and picked up the garbage were the untouchables. Shopkeepers were another class; soldiers of different kinds that were easily identifiable; the Sikhs all wore their turbans, at least they looked like the Sikhs in the movies. Each one had to have a knife of some kind in his turban. Also, the taxi cab drivers, who drove old-style sedans, 4-door topless cars, were Sikhs. The British had the best soldiers, which were Gurkhas. The average Gurkha was about 5 feet 5 inches tall and carried a great big curved knife. They were reputably the best fighters that the British had anywhere in the world.

We had ten days to spend in Calcutta. We started right out the next day, the group of nine of us that had crossed the country together, to see as much of the city as we possibly could, and learn something about the country. The only city we had seen before was Karachi, and Calcutta was very different. One good thing about the English was that the newspaper was published in English, the <u>Calcutta Times</u>, which we regularly read. It was circulated in the whole country, so it was probably the only newspaper in all of India that anybody, no matter where they were, could read. Anybody who had been to school and worked for the English knew enough to read the paper.

We went to places like the Hindu Sect, Jain Temple. It was a very large and elaborate temple which covered a block or more of different buildings. It was not like any church you ever saw. We also took a boat ride down a branch of the Ganges River to the famous (at least they told us they were) Botanical Gardens, which had several hundreds of different kinds of plants and trees. We also saw Fakirs on street corners who were snake charmers with the cobras in the basket. They were entertaining and passed the hat for donations. In one case, we gave a rupee or two enough for the snake charmer to let a mongoose out of his box, and we saw the mongoose fight the cobra. As usual, the mongoose won; the cobra could not strike him as the mongoose was too quick, and finally got the cobra by the head, and hung on until the cobra was done in completely. There were also plenty of holy men around, acres of Fakirs in India, and thousands of beggars all over, most of them belonging to a beggar caste, where as children, they are mutilated by the family, like having their legs tied back behind their heads, so that they would grow that way from babies on, and some with their arms tied in knots that grew into hideous combinations. It was surprising how some of them have learned to get around and live on the few annas that people give them.

On the boat trip to the Botanical Gardens, we passed a large U.S. ammunition dump, and assumed that's where they stored a lot of the stuff from our liberty ship. I would say it covered fifty acres, and full of bombs of all kinds, and as far as I know, none of them were ever used in the war in that part of the world.

One of the things we went to see that was not very pleasant were the burning ghats, where the dead were cremated. The proper wood was mango, which doesn't have much ash left after it is burned. On a cement platform alongside the river, a pile of mango wood was made, and the body, fully clothed, was placed on it and they burned all day. According to the people we talked to there, it was not uncommon for a man's widow to be thrown on the fire with him when he was cremated. This was known as "sutee", which had been outlawed by the English years ago, but still went on. I can't imagine any living widow, who would want to be thrown on a fire with her dead husband, probably with her feet and hands tied together, especially when the older men in India often had very young wives. Many of the marriages were arranged when the girls were only two or three years old. Then they had to live up to it, and bring a large-sized dowry with them. No woman could get married without a dowry, so many of them wore it on their arms with gold bangles up to the elbow while they were looking for a husband. We saw the burning ghats, on the Ganges banks, and what I couldn't understand and never will, was that once the fire was out and only the ashes left, they were thrown into the sacred river. The river was also full of people bathing, washing their clothes, taking jars of water out of the river and using it not only to wash but to drink. They claimed that nobody had ever gotten sick from drinking water from the sacred Ganges, although it was also used for everything, including a sewer.

As usual, we spent a good deal of time finding places to eat, and found a couple that catered to the English but also to American soldiers, who had more money than anybody else. One was the Grand Hotel in Calcutta, which had a nice dining room. The other was a restaurant famous for the British called Firpo's. I still have a menu that I kept from it that had things like a chota peg of whisky (scotch) for one rupee. Chota peg meant about half a shot; beef steak was listed as three rupees, two annas, approximately a dollar. We ate there several times, and had quite a few pegs of whisky. The bad side of Calcutta was the poverty and the number of people that were starving, children with swollen stomachs, almost everybody, it seemed, on the streets begging, their hands out and saying bachees saab (gift). There wasn't a block that I can remember passing where there were not people who had died of starvation. Someone would then come and pull their clothing, (dhoti) up over their head, and push them up against a wall. I remember walking around the block where the Red Cross unit we stayed in was, and in that block, there were eight or nine bodies. The <u>Calcutta Times</u> daily reported the number of bodies picked up, which was in the thousands, and that the average body laid there for three days before being picked up. It gave you an eerie feeling like you were walking through a morgue much of the time.

Like all cities of that size and the times, streets were full of prostitutes and pimps of all sizes, shapes, and so forth. They were often very persistent – you had to practically hit them over the head to get them not to chase you and keep propositioning you. I remember one because I was involved and not in the way you might think. There was a teen-aged boy with two other children, his sister and a smaller boy. The sister was nine or ten and the third child was a little boy about six. He accosted three of us in a group, offering his sister for two rupees. We then told him 'no' and he reduced it to one rupee and told us he had a place we could go with them, and after finally getting rid of him, or so we thought, he started offering his little brother for 3 annas. At this point, I had listened enough, so I grabbed him and gave him a long lecture on the immorality of what he was doing, that he had no right to sell his sister and brother to anybody, that they were human beings just like he was, and he certainly had no right to sell them on the street to anybody for anything could happen to them. He pled poverty of course, and said they hadn't eaten in two days, so I gave him some more of my lecture that one person doesn't own another and they can't peddle them on the streets that way, and then I gave him five rupees which was a large amount to him, about a dollar and sixty cents in our money. He told his sister and brother that he would take them to a street vendor that was around the corner and would see that they got all they wanted to eat. At least I tried.

There was a very famous prostitute in Calcutta, said to be a Hindu princess of the highest caste who was known as Hundred Rupee Mary. She was even famous in the United States, and had been written up in Time magazine in the U.S., as entertaining soldiers from Pvt. to General and all ranks in between. In India, a hundred rupees was more than a lot of the population earned in a year. Someone I knew couldn't resist. So, he went to see Hundred Rupee Mary, and when he returned, everybody asked him what had happened. His story simply was that it was a lovely mansion-like house, he paid his hundred rupees to the attendant, and waited his turn for fifteen or twenty minutes. Then, he proceeded to the room where Hundred Rupee Mary was. He said that shortly after he started, she reached over to the table next to her, grabbed a mango, and ate it, finishing at the same time as he finished his goal. He was rather let down.

I wanted to see the famous Black Hole of Calcutta, where a hundred Englishmen had died when they were thrown into this very small room back in the nineteenth century. Of Indians that we talked to and cab drivers, even the rickshaw pullers, no one would admit to knowing where it was (although I have since seen the descriptions of the place and where it is). I guess the Indians were not very proud of it and the British certainly made them pay many times over.

As an example of how the British treated the Indians was my purchase of a pair of short pants. I went to a clothing store and found some shorts that would fit me, probably a size 28 in those days. They were khaki shorts, and the merchant offered them to me for nine, maybe ten rupees. Having been told that you always bargained in places like that, I did my best and got him down to seven rupees, at which I was satisfied and bought the shorts for $2.10. About the time I was ready to leave, a British corporal came in and looked at the shorts, took a pair out of the same pile that I had just gotten one from for seven rupees, and he looked at the proprietor, called him a few names, like a "fucking wog", and said "what do you want for these?" The storekeeper, with a straight face, simply said he wanted five rupees. The British soldier then called him a "bloody thief" and a few other choice names and said, "Here, I'll give you four rupees and you're lucky to get those." He threw four rupees at him, took the shorts, and left. The storekeeper said "thank you, sahib" to the Englishman as he left. I didn't even get a "thank you" for my seven rupees for the identical shorts I had purchased.

These were the main things we saw in Calcutta. It was very depressing, with the starvation, the poor, and the thing that disturbed me, was no sign of children playing anywhere. In other countries, you often see groups of children under ten, playing in the streets. Children will play tag, chase each other, laugh and carry on – I never saw any sign of humor in the Indians. I think it's probably they're afraid they'll play with someone of the wrong caste. I also asked a couple of Indians that spoke good English asking them why the caste system was so important to them. Several of them had caste marks on their foreheads; the Brahmans had a red mark on their forehead, and other castes had a blue one put on their forehead. I asked one why the really poor or low caste people simply didn't move to another town and get a red dot (one of the highest castes) tattooed on their foreheads. He was completely horrified by this idea, you couldn't do that, it wouldn't be right, no one would leave their caste. You were born in a caste and you stayed in it and you didn't want to change it.

    I learned a few things about India and our ten days in Calcutta came to an end too soon, and we had to report to a Transportation Officer. Before leaving Calcutta, I have one final note of a not too pleasant subject. Many of the beggars in the streets in Calcutta were lepers, who had the most horrendous disfigurations that you could imagine, including arms or legs that were just bloody stumps and sores. This brings to one's mind when you see it some understanding of why lepers were always treated so badly, even in many mentions in the Bible. If there was anything that Jesus cured, it was certainly a great thing when He cured lepers.

    That was the end of Calcutta and we were about to start on a train for upper Assam, for transportation to China.

8. TRANSPORT TO CHINA

Transportation to upper Assam and to China began in Calcutta on a pretty good sized train, although a different gage than the trains we had come across India from Karachi. As usual, after a little screaming at the Indian train agents, we managed a first-class compartment for the first stage of the trip. We left early in the morning, and headed to the north first, and then east on the train. It seemed the train stopped every 15 or 20 minutes at a station. About four o'clock in the afternoon, we came to the end of this particular train line. The train stopped at a station, and about a block away and up ahead was another train line with a narrower gage than the one we had been on. When we got up there, there was a passenger train, with mostly wooden passenger cars. The train was being held up, as the first car on the train behind the engine, a first-class car, was occupied by ten or eleven South African soldiers. They were a wild bunch, you could tell by talking to them, and hearing some of their stories. They were as rough as they come, and would have made a Texan blush. The train was held up was because they wouldn't get out of the first-class compartment when the Indian army train station officer ordered them to. They claimed he had no authority over them, that they were not British Army or British Indian Army; they were South African Army, and their badges proved it. To strengthen their cause for the first-class compartment, they invited all nine of us GIs to join them. We gladly did, not only to support them and ride first-class some more, but also because they had an ample supply of bottled Indian beer, which they gladly swapped with us for cigarettes. Like anybody in the world, at that time anyway, everybody wanted American cigarettes and we had plenty of them in our bags. So, the train agent left for a while (the train couldn't leave until he gave the okay) and we sat there for a couple of hours. The station agent came back a couple of times during that two-hours, and argued some more. Finally, the South Africans agreed to move back one car to a second-class car simply so the train would go. The train left after we finally moved. They had to move a lot of people out of the second-class car to turn it over to us, but finally on we steamed.

Late into the night, all of the trains stopped for several hours, and for what I have no idea. The next day, around noon, we reached the end of the line for that particular train. The end of it was right at the edge of the Brahmaputra River. It was the largest river I had ever seen, it made the Mississippi look small. It is the largest river in India. The banks of it were maybe 200 feet high. The river was at low water, like a stream in the middle of a valley, and it was still at least a mile or so wide, and this was at a time of drought. We had lost our South African friends earlier in the day so we had to unload everything we owned. So we shouldered our carbines and carried all our stuff down a fairly steep bank, maybe four or five blocks long and followed a path to where there was a ferryboat with a gangplank out to it. It took one across the river, which took fifteen minutes. Then on the other side of the river, we had to repeat the performance of climbing up the bank of the river, where there was a new train.

We stayed on this new train until the end of the line. It was a very narrow gage, all wooden cars, and quite ancient. The engine looked like something from the early part of the twentieth century, it was an all-steam train. The passenger car was just wooden benches along both sides, and no windows, but wooden shutters for all the windows and for the doors at both ends of the car, for reasons I will explain a little bit later. It was a very narrow track, maybe 28 to 30 inches wide, sort of a "Hooterville trolley" type.

We boarded this small train, maybe a dozen cars on it. All of the cars, including ours, were packed with local people, and the train seemed to stopped every 10 minutes at a station. Perhaps an hour into the trip, the train came to a stop before the next station. You could see the station perhaps a half a mile ahead, with banyan trees next to it. The train stopped about 500 yards before the station, the train employees came along and carefully shuttered each car, lowering all the shutters and making sure they were bolted down. The doors of each car were locked so that no one could get out or get into the train. After the train was thoroughly sealed up, it slowly pulled up to the station. As soon as the train stopped at the station, a few thousand monkeys jumped out of the banyan trees and swarmed on the train. Apparently, they did this all the time, and on any car they could break into, the people inside were immediately attacked and anything to eat was taken. It was a raid by over a thousand monkeys. Some of the people inside the cars, including the Indian natives, had sticks to hit the monkeys if they were able to reach through the shutters. After a bit, with the aid of these sticks, the back end of the train was unloaded, and the train took off, and all the monkeys jumped off and went back to the banyan trees. My best guess was there must have been about five thousand monkeys in the trees.

We went on through the jungle, like I had never seen before, it was truly a jungle, with the train slowly moving. We stopped at another station, with no problems, and then continued on for another hour. At the next stop, we went through the monkey situation again, stopping way before the station, and sealing all the cars. When we stopped at the station, we were beset by a few thousand more monkeys from a couple of large trees nearby. The monkeys did not look a bit friendly, but none of them got into our car.

We were now in the part of India known as Assam, a wild jungle and full of large tea plantations, where some of the greatest teas in the world were grown on the British plantations. You can still find Assam tea occasionally here. We made lots of stops until we finally reached the end of the line, which was a town called Dibrugarh.

The management of freight there was done by American railroad men and it was the only time I ever saw trains with up to 20 cars loose shunted (no power). To get them going fast; they just pushed them away and headed them towards the right switch. There were maybe 20 train tracks with trains of different kinds of cargo on them, being loose shunted with engineers looking like they were having great fun. Railroad cars occasionally went a little past the stop or hit the stop too hard, but these guys were pretty good at it.

Anyway, we finally got out of the train, and I am glad to say we were picked up by a GI, 4 x 6 standard Army truck, and taken to a camp about five miles from the Chabua airport, which was the main airport for people who flew into China. The camp was made out of bamboo buildings and lots of tents. This was about late February, the best time I can place it now, late February or early March. I didn't mark the dates down in my records, and I wasn't writing any letters at this time. We arrived from Dibrugarh to Chabua after traveling about an hour in the truck.

So, it was probably 25 to 30 miles from the end of the road to this camp near the airfield.

In early 1944, the Japanese marched up the Malay Peninsula into Burma with almost no opposition of any kind. In late February, the British did send one group, which got to be well-known, perhaps the only one with any chance of stopping the Japanese at Rangoon or even before. These were known as the Chindits, who marched in late February, and they were led by a famous general, Orde Wingate. These were both British and Indian troops mixed together. Wingate was killed in an air crash in March 1944. Wingate's foray into Burma was important in one sense, in that it was the first time for an Army to invade another country completely supplied by air, with bombers, transport planes, gliders, etc. The Americans supplied the air support for Wingate's troops, and it was under the control of Colonel Phillip Cochran.

Most of the time in the camp near Chabua airfield, we were waiting to fly into China and had nothing to do except sit around and tell each other lies about the good life back home. The Japanese were more successful. They had, by then, marched all the way through Burma. They had taken Mandalay back in 1942, and now they were at Mandalay, Rangoon, and Lashio, which was the start of the old Burma Road. By now, the end of February and beginning of March 1944, the Japanese were knocking on the door of India, at Imphal and Kohima. The fear was that if they took these two towns, India was open to attack and Upper Assam would be lost. In Assam we were starting construction on the Ledo Road, which would connect to the old Burma Road to China. Incidentally, I found no records of it ever, but there was an Indian army marching north in Burma and up to the border of India that was a renegade Indian army with 15,000 soldiers led by an Indian general who had joined the Japanese side of the war. (Don't put that one in your history books, as no records exist.)

When the Japanese were getting close to Imphal and Kohima, the British were digging in and, at the time, not successful in stopping the Japanese advance. We were put on red alert and were told we would have to go down and join the English troops fighting at Kohima. We had to figure out what we needed in our field packs, clothing, carbines, and so forth. We were issued 500 rounds of ammunition per man and told to be ready. If called, we had 30 minutes to join the actual shooting war. I can't say that we looked forward to it, but had we been ordered, we would have gone, of course. Nothing happened though, and we never got called. What did happen was that in India at the time all U.S. cargo airplanes were pulled off the China run and went all over India picking up Gurkha troops. They brought them to the Indian and English troops that were fighting and in desperate need of support. With the support from the Gurkhas, the battle was finally won and the Japanese army never got into India. But it got awful darn close, close enough to almost have gotten me into it. We had few interesting visitors to our Chabua camp. Some of them were Tibetans who came down from the mountains; and according to my maps at the time, we were much closer to Lhasa, the capital of Tibet, than to Kunming. You could see the mountains all around, snow-capped Himalayas. People were always saying that's Tibet in that direction, pointing north. Tibetans on their way to Burma and other places often stopped by with their trading skins. Even in the hot weather, their clothes were half fur. You could also tell when a Tibetan was coming from at least a block away. As Tibetans never believed in taking baths; what they did was rub their skin regularly and all over with rancid yak butter. None of them spoke English and none of us knew any Tibetan. Everybody shook hands but nobody liked the smell.

We also had several visits from people that were claimed to still be headhunters from the foothills of the mountains between Assam and China, known as the Naga Hills tribesmen. Every one of them seemed to have about 15 knives in his garments, ranging from 3 or 4 inches in length to 18 inches. They were certainly ferocious looking, but never caused any trouble, they just came and bowed and said hello, so to speak.

We did have one interesting visit from a Hindu Fakir, a holy man, who came to collect for money. For a total of 10 rupees, his aides dug a big hole, maybe 14 inches deep. Then he took off his turban and tightly wrapped it around his whole head, from the neck to the top, he tied it tight, and stuck his head in the hole, and his aides shoveled all the dirt they had dug out of the hole, around his head. When they didn't have enough, they dug some more. They got help from quite a few of the GIs, not me, mind you, and went stomping down the dirt to make sure that he was well buried in the dirt from shoulders down and from the shoulders up, he was in the air. After the GIs had finished trampling the dirt to make sure it was really packed down, there was no way anybody could breathe through it, then they packed some more. He then straightened up his body into the air and his body walked around in a circle, switching from side to side and never turning his neck. According to my watch, he stayed that way for almost 20 minutes. He was buried alive, head first in the dirt. Then his aides started digging and got him out; he unwrapped the turban from his head and he was fine. How he held his breath for 20 minutes, I will never know. Maybe the Japanese pearl-diving women could learn something from him or maybe he learned it from them, I don't know, but it was quite a show.

One time when I was thoroughly bored and had nothing to read to speak of and tired of my associates and their stories, I decided to take a hike in the jungle. I wandered out of camp, ran into an animal path and I wandered down it through the jungle for about half an hour, about a couple of miles from the camp. I went around a bend of this three to four feet wide path, and sometimes narrower, with jungle twice as high as I was and that was just the grass; the trees were much bigger. Anyway, when I went around the corner there I was face-to-face with a wild elephant. He had no signs on him of ever being captured, no foot chains, etc. that captured elephants had. I looked at the elephant and he looked at me. I did a 180 degree turn; the walk that had taken me nearly an hour to make into the jungle, I made back in, I think 60 seconds. You never saw me move so fast. I never saw the elephant again, nor he me.

Warnings were posted on the bulletin board in the camp, and one I remember said if you had to go to the latrine in the night, to always be sure to take a flashlight and not to go unless you had to, but when you do, take a flashlight because the area was full of cobras. In India, a lot of them were quite large. I had noticed in the Calcutta Times that the paper published the number of Indians that had been killed by cobra bites and there were over ten thousand a year. Quite a few GIs refused to go to the latrine, which was only maybe 150 to 200 feet away from the tents. Some people would endure it, but who would want to run into a cobra.

A cobra would be worse than a tiger, which were also in the area. I didn't see any tigers though.

There was nearby a small British fighter plane field with Hawker Hurricanes, single-engine fighter planes. They were nothing fancy like the British Spitfires. The pilots would take off and when they got maybe 50 feet in the air, they would head out over Burma and a couple of hours later, they would come back. After they had a successful attack of dropping small bombs on Japanese troops, they would do loops and barrel rolls and then land. It was sort of a free air show about three times a week.

The only really bad thing that happened to me in Upper Assam was my first major attack of stomach trouble. After I had been there about three weeks, not thinking about the food, I started having very bad stomach pains and everything that went with it. It just left me completely doubled over and could only moan and groan. After a couple of days, I went to the dispensary, talked to a doctor who happened to be from the University of Chicago, and he simply said that I had dysentery of some kind and it was quite common. The only thing he could do was to help me get back into the dispensary ward where there were about 5 beds. As he gave me strong tea, I asked him if the tea would relieve these pains and he said that there wasn't anything they could give me to help. They did have some sulfa, but it was for the troops who had STDs, which was virulent forms of gonorrhea in Burma. All the sulfa they had was used to treat that. There was a soldier who was ambulatory but he had picked up the Burmese variety from a Burma girl and he had one book that he carried around in his pocket. It was <u>The Rubyiat of Omar Khyam</u>, the Fitzgerald English translation, with 120 verses of it. He had been there for so long with so little to do that he had memorized, in order, the complete 120 verses, and would recite them at the drop of a hat to anybody that showed the slightest interest in them. You just never know who you will meet in the army.

He caught his disease on working on the Ledo Road (he was a supervisor of some kind), which was the road being built from Upper Assam down into Burma to connect with the old Burma Road at Myitkyina. I didn't realize until later how segregated our army was; he said almost all the people building the road and doing the menial jobs like driving trucks and operating machinery were all black. According to him (the doctor supported him on this one), at least 50% of the American troops working on this road either got malaria or the Burmese STD. They also had to clear the worst part of the jungle, with all the rain and terrible battles with leeches. A hot cigarette usually got rid of a leech on you. No matter where you go, you can learn something.

After six days in this dispensary ward, a friend from the group I had traveled all the way from California, came by and told me they were shipping out the next day for Kunming. I said hey, wait for me and they said, sorry, we're gone. There was nothing I could do about it. When the doctor showed up the next morning, I immediately started after him to get me out of there and to get me to Kunming so I could get there with my compatriots. He said he didn't know but he would see what he could do. He finally came back the next day, after going to headquarters, wherever that was, and said he had arranged for me to fly in two days to Kunming on a hospital flight, on a C-47. I could be put on that flight and it was only for patients.

9. A GREAT FLIGHT

Later, I was picked up in a truck and taken to the Chabua airfield and driven to a bright shiny aluminum C-47 (DC-3). It wasn't one painted olive drab like the regular Air Force planes. This was for seven patients like me riding along to Kunming. The only markings on this shiny DC-3 were large red crosses on it. Both sides of the fuselage, as well as on the wings, top and bottom, to indicate that this was a hospital ship. Shortly after we were airborne, the captain came back and told us that since this was such a beautiful day (if my memory is right, either the last day of March or the first day of April), it was clear and no storms. We flew over jungle for about an hour, maybe two thousand feet in the air. After a while, we were able to see a lot of the work being done on the Ledo Road, there were only about 20 miles completed by then; we flew over the lush Burmese jungle and finally came upon a town that was occupied by the Japanese, which happened to be Myitkyina, a most important point. We could see the airfield with Japanese bombers on it. Japanese troops were marching around the town and we flew over, maybe a thousand feet above them, and some of the Japanese looked like they were waving at us. The captain waggled his wings back and forth at them and he said he had done this several times before and no shots had ever been fired at him. We then started flying through valleys (and this was a great pilot). We were anywhere from one to two thousand feet (seldom more) above the valley floor. On both sides of us but particularly on the north side, were mountains that went up to 20,000 feet. A few of them, the tallest ones, you couldn't see the tops because they were in the clouds. They were just a few thousand feet above where we were; and were covered with snow and ice. When we got to the end of one valley, we followed a trail around and we'd see a lot of the old Burma Road. These mountain sights were the most spectacular and awesome I'd ever imagined and no one else I know had gone to Kunming this way. The usual and shorter route was 20,000+ feet over the mountains and in clouds most of the way. This flight on a rare clear day was a thrill I'll never forget.

Down another valley, we really followed the Burma Road all the way to Kunming, and a good many valleys with more spectacular mountains – I couldn't believe – I almost lost my eyes trying to see more of the gorgeous mountains that loomed 10,000 feet to 20,000 feet above you. It was spectacular – breathtaking and unforgettable. As far as I know from all I have met, etc., in China I was the only non Air Force person to get there by the great scenic route. The others all flew over the "hump" either at night or in the clouds at 20,000 feet.

Finally, we went into a cloud and when we came out of the clouds, there was Lake Kunming, at least that's the only name I ever heard it called, a large lake, maybe five to six miles long and a big airport, and that was Kunming. We landed smoothly, I might add; the whole trip had probably taken about five hours.

We landed and pulled up in front of a white shack that was about 40 feet long and 18 feet deep with a regular style roof on it and a sign on the roof right in front of where the double doors were that said simply "Kunming, China altitude 6240. So, my first knowledge direct of China was the altitude of Kunming – 6,240 feet.

10. CHINA – FIRST OF 600 DAYS

After we landed in China and were greeted by the sign on the airport operations shack that said "Kunming, China altitude 6,240 feet", the first thing that grabs you when you get there is how difficult it is to breathe at 6,240 feet altitude when you're used to being close to sea level – not only recently but most of your life. People said not to worry and in a month you won't know the difference. I don't think it took that long but it certainly makes a difference when you walk about two blocks and are completely out of breath, even though you're twenty-one years old and in good shape. Actually, I was twenty-two then – barely.

The other noticeable thing in the beginning, is the minute you get on the ground in that part of China (maybe all of it), is the odor. China has a distinct odor everywhere that I went (at least in southwestern China), due to the fact that for 2,000 years or more, from every piece of land as big as a card table to farms of many acres, has been fertilized for 2,000 or more years with human waste. (what the Chinese called nightsoil because they left the buckets to be picked up early each morning in the front of their houses. It's a very strong, acrid, fecal, any word you can think of that really describes the odor. Another adjective to add but it's one that takes you quite a while to get used to – one that you never get rid of and one, depending on where you're staying, you get much stronger versions of it as the so-called "honey-dippers" carts go by. These are carts with large barrels of maybe 300 to 400 gallons in size, with an open top and are pulled by a pony. They drive down the streets, picking up and dumping the nightsoil from the houses. They then go out to the country with this and have a dipper like bucket on the end of an eight foot pole which was then dipped in the bucket and then carefully poured around each plant in the field. If there's nothing growing, they just pour it all over the field and when they have things growing, the dipper puts a small amount from the dipper by each single plant. It shows you what people do when they have lots more people being employed even though they don't pay them much. That has to be the worst job in the world, or at least the worst smelling job, with horse carts coming by with the "honey bucket." You can smell them half a mile away. It doesn't seem to bother the locals; they just grow up with it.

Those were the first two things I noticed. The third thing I noticed because it was such a contrast from India was that in many places, there were groups of children playing and laughing and running and yelling and pushing, as kids will; something I found so missing from the places I had been to in India. The Chinese people were all laughing and even the first ones you saw acted like they were glad to see you. Every Chinese soldier saluted every American he saw, no matter what the American rank was or what he was doing.

11. KUNMING – MY JOB

Having landed at Kunming Airport, I didn't know it was going to be my work home which is how it turned out. We were taken by truck to another camp with lots of tents, (what the Army called six-man tents) room for six – eight if you stretched it, with Army cots next to Hostel One, which was the headquarters for the ground Y-Force, which was headed by a general known as "Pinky" Dorn. He had walked out of Burma with General Stilwell as a captain when the Japs chased the American Army out of Burma in 1942. Anyway, Stilwell's famous quote was "we got the hell kicked out of us." They struggled through Rangoon, Mandalay and all the way to India through the jungles under terrible and starving conditions.

We were supposed to be sent to Kweilin, China, about 500 to 600 miles to the east but soon after I landed in China, the Japanese decided they didn't want anything more going on in that area. They swept from Hong Kong, which they had already taken in December 1941, and moved south and took the rest of the China coast all the way down to French-Indo-China, including at the time, only three or four airfields. One was at Kweilin, which was going to be the headquarters for Z-Force.

One of my friends who was evacuated before the Japanese got to Kweilin, complained about having to burn up a warehouse full of U.S. Air Force leather jackets. He wanted to take one to wear but they had burn them all up so that the Japanese pilots couldn't have them.

We did little when we camped next to Hostel One in Kunming except have a few lectures about Chinese culture. Then for the second time, my health got the better of me and I came down with the same kind of dysentery that I had had in Assam. I was completely unable to do anything except moan and wish I was dead – I felt so bad. Finally, after a couple of more days of it, I went on sick call and went to the dispensary and got the same results as in India. They put me in a ward-like tent with people as sick as I was and a houseboy gave us tea day and night. I lay on a cot for about four days drinking strong tea brought by the Chinese attendant. The tea did quiet me down in about four days and I insisted they turn me loose so I could at least get assigned somewhere. When I got out, I immediately looked for the people I had traveled with before, and most of them had already been given jobs – some of them who had gone to Kweilin were already on their way back – they had burned supplies there.

I did nothing for several days, and by the postings on the bulletin board on who is supposed to do what, I was posted on "detached service" to Y-Force Air Freight, which meant I had a job. The next day, I arrived to work at the airport where a major was in charge. In the original plan, we were to work around the clock. We were used to working 8-hour shifts and there were few problems with working round the clock. At that time in 1944, the airplanes did not fly supplies over the "hump" at night. All supplies came in roughly from 11:00 in the morning to 5:00 at night and had to be stored until the next day when they could be delivered. The major was supposed to come in every day and sign for the supplies' air manifests, which he did for only 2 or 3 days. The next day when he came in, he had me go with him and see how they start to work at 6:30 in the morning. So, the next day as he came in, he told me to sign the aircraft manifest for each cargo planeload, and I signed them for him with my name. A day later, he told me in the evening not to worry that

I was to sign them and not to think about saving him a lot of work. He wouldn't be in the following morning. He never came back another morning; the other two people who were supposed to be assigned there disappeared and there I was alone with all the stuff the Air Force had brought in. For all the rest of my time in China I had no CO (commanding officer). My status was simply "detached" service from Z-Force to Y-Force to Service of Supply (SOS). Y and Z-Forces were abandoned when Stillwell was recalled. The GIs who worked for me were "unassigned" too. There was no Air Freight section on any table of organization. When people asked for my CO, I just referred them to the SOS General.

Everything brought in was dumped into a warehouse at the edge of the airport and I was given the job of seeing that whatever they brought was sent to the right warehouse depot of which there were half a dozen around the area. There was one for ammunition, one for fuel, and for quartermaster supplies, including clothing; a medical depot and another for engineering and vehicles. Thus, there were six or seven different places a truck had to be filled for delivery. The trucks I had were two old Burma Road trucks which had been converted I don't know when, but somewhere in the past, to run on charcoal gas. (Many cars in Europe ran that way during the war.) They looked like water heaters with burners attached to the back end of these trucks, and generated gas by burning charcoal for the engine. Each truck had a driver and an assistant. The assistant had to start the motor in the truck with maybe a half cup of gasoline or kerosene put into the carburetor. Once it started, it was luck to switch over to the gas from the gas generator. Sometimes it took several tries to do it. Also, the trucks had to be cranked by hand, which the assistant did. My job was to put a load together with the supplies. If I had two truckloads, I would take the two trucks with a pass I signed to get off the airport by the airport Chinese Army Guards. That was an experience where I was welcomed by gravel roads full of big holes. The trucks were painted and marked on the sides "YBHTA" which was the Yunan Burma Highway Transportation Association. They were in pretty bad shape. I don't know how many hundred thousand miles were on them, but they were held together with wire and string. To this day, I can remember in the first month or two with something like seven DC-3 loads (C-47) per day. At that altitude and the distance they had to fly from one of the Assam bases about 700 miles away and they could only carry up to 3,500 pounds of cargo. When I got seven airplanes, I got 25,000 pounds of cargo which, with luck meant about 8-10 loads, so with these two old trucks, I sorted and delivered all our supplies.

There were five air fields in Upper Assam that all shipped goods to Kunming, which was the main point of entry for all American goods for China. The five airports in Upper Assam that shipped supplies with ATC were as follows: Chabua, Tezpur, Dinjan, Jorhat, and Sookerating. I had planes coming, with cargo from those five different fields. I signed the manifest for receiving all the cargo that was assigned to the ground forces. The great bulk of the cargo that was flown to China went to the Air Force, which ended up at a different part of the air field. The C-47s carried anywhere from 2,500 to a maximum of maybe 3,400 pounds, which was not a lot of cargo, but enough to take a few hundred Chinese laborers, (coolies that they were called by everybody) to unload the airplanes and then bring it to the warehouse and unload them onto the floor, where I then had to sort out what went where, load them back on different trucks, (my YBHTA trucks) and then personally escort them (one or two of them together) to a depot warehouse. That essentially was my job that expanded as time went on in China.

The first thing I noted because it was so different, was that there t were literally thousands of Chinese working on the field. They were extending the runway and everything was done by hand. Alongside the runway, in many places were big piles of rock. Beside each pile of rock which was a pile maybe four feet high and ten feet across from side of the runway spaced out one pile every 100 or 200 yards. There were anywhere from 20 to as many as 100 people, men, women, children, old folks, and all – each person was equipped with two things, a hammer and a circle of rope approximately 2 ½ to 3 inches in diameter. They grabbed a big hunk of rock and started pounding on it. You pounded until you broke off a piece small enough to fit through the circle of rope. They were the gravel making machines – human gravel-making machines. They were making rocks, which were then scooped up and dumped on the end of the runway. They were working to make the runway a mile long so it could accommodate bigger airplanes. The runway wasn't long enough so we didn't have any B-17s flying fortresses. They were all in England, I guess. The gravel was taken to the end of the runway and then was rolled into it. It was about 40 yards wide, only room enough for one cargo plane to land. The rollers were great big stones, maybe eight or ten feet high and had been made round like a rolling pin, with a hole in the center with a rope through it. The rope then stretched out and joined itself at maybe 50 or 100 feet past the roller. This big rolling pin was then pulled by at least six to seven hundred Chinese coolies to slowly roll the gravel into the runway. This building of a runway a mile long took an awful lot of labor paid for by the United States Government.

I tried to get to know as much as I could from friends in Chunking at Headquarters who told me that the United States Government was charged for the labor for everything we did. Any Chinese labor we used was paid for in American dollars at the official rate of exchange, which I believe was either five or ten Chinese National dollars to American dollars. On the open market, the free rate was anywhere from 100 to 200 Chinese Nationals, so the American Government was paying the Chinese anywhere from 10 to 25 times as much as they needed to have paid. That was one way Chiang Kai-shek, took the Americans in all kinds of ways. General Stilwell disliked him, and called him "Peanut", but most GIs preferred a more pejorative term – he was known as "Shanker Jack". I don't think Generalissimo would like that, but he made millions of dollars for himself. Most of it was from our government. I did not see the big airbase they were working on at Chengdu for B-29s, which were going to fly from there to Japan. It took an airfield of 6,000 feet or more for the B-29s. We were told there were at least 100,000 Chinese building that airfield, an airfield that turned out very quickly, not to be any good. It was too far from Japan for the B-29s to carry a decent load, and the gas, they needed to go to Tokyo and back. They made a very small number of test raids to learn this in early 1945. They quickly learned that the base in Guam was closer to Japan. That is where all the B-29s flew out of, including the Enola Gay.

The airport at Kunming was my home, so to speak, for at least 8 or 10 hours a day, six days a week. Nobody worked on Sunday, by the way, including the Japanese, but also the U.S.

Air Transport Command until the Air Force became a separate branch of the service under the command of General Tunner.

12. THE HUMP

The Hump was the direct flight from Upper Assam's five small airports, (the main one being Chabua) over the Himalaya Mountains, to Kunming. It was approximately, as I recall, usually listed at about 700 miles. The highest peak on the maps, anyway, was Mount Tali, which was almost 22,000 feet high, and usually the instructions were to fly around it, not over it. The planes, primarily in the beginning, were all DC-3s (or C-47s), cargo models, and they carried something slightly less than 2 tons because of the altitude they had to reach. The preferred altitude which took considerable time to reach, was about 20,000 feet. If they could get that high, they were sure not to run into any mountains, but it added to the time. Also, the weather over the hump was said to be the worst in the world, with continual storms and downdrafts, where the plane would suddenly drop several thousand feet – very bad weather. The pilots tended to be very young, as young as I was, or younger, nineteen to twenty-three years old. An old one was twenty-five years old, and many of them were said to have very little experience in flying in that kind of weather in those transport planes. Some of the pilots were said to have as little as 150 hours of total flying time before they suddenly found themselves flying over the hump, which may be why the accident record was pretty bad. I remember talking to pilots who said that on a clear day, which over the hump was pretty rare, but that on a clear day you didn't need to worry about your navigation, you could simply fly from one burned out spot to the next, where planes had crashed. During the whole war, the only figures I ever heard were that the hump cost the United States Air Corps somewhere between

600 to 800 airplanes. That was a lot of wrecks and a lot of loss of Americans.

The hump route had first been flown by the Chinese National Air Corporation (CNAC), which was a private corporation, flew from Calcutta, with a stop in Assam, and over the hump to China, starting around 1940. It was a private company, said to be 49% owned and staffed, with planes from Pan American (the United States overseas well-known airline). The other 51% of CNAC, according to one of their pilots that I got to know, was owned by Madam Soong, the wife of Generalissimo Chiang Kai-shek. Madam Soong was very popular in the United States, a sort of semi-ambassador from China and her family was one of the richest in China. She was married to the Generalissimo, the dictator of Nationalist China. She was a Wellsley graduate and spent a lot of time in the United States, spoke perfect English, and was a "friend" of President Roosevelt. It is said that when she came to America, many times she stayed in the White House, and had a lot of political influence. One of her brothers was also the Chinese ambassador to the United States in the 1940's. She and her husband were also pretty good friends with General Chennault, who at one time on leave from the American Army, was in charge of all Chinese airplanes and airports around 1939 or 1940.

Back in the 1930's, (1936 or 1937) when the Japanese went to war in China, they conquered everything fairly easily, and the usual view, at least in Kunming, when I was there, was that the Chinese had fought the Japanese in 1938, which was long before we got there. When the knowledge of Pearl Harbor was circulated, there was great rejoicing in Chunking, then capital of China. The feeling was that they didn't have to worry about the war any more. The Americans would come and win it for them, and that's the way it turned out in the long run. You get a lot of politics thrown in, but these were all pretty well known facts, at least where I was.

The hump was flying over the Himalayas to Kunming was necessary because up until the Japanese occupied most of Burma in 1942, the main route to China had been (the only route for supplies or people) through Burma and then on the Burma Road. Most supplies entered Burma from ships at Rangoon. They were also shipped by train to Mandalay and from Mandalay, the train lines ran up to the northeastern area of Burma, to the town of Lashio. At Lashio, the Burma Road started and continued through Burma to the Chinese border and to Yunan Province and Kunming. Most of the road was built on the side of the mountains, that it went up to 8,000 feet, where the trucks had to drive up and down and around – it was quite a trip. The distance, as I recall, was usually quoted somewhere around 750 miles, maybe a little less. Once the Japanese occupied Lashio and a town very near the border of China, Myitkyina, the supply line to China was cut completely except for a small amount that CNAC then flew over the Hump, maybe a couple of airplane loads a day.

There I was, at the end of March, first of April, collecting all the goods that were shipped to the Y-Forces, the ground forces in China.

The Y-Forces had been created by Brigadier General Joseph Stilwell, as part of his long-range plan to fight the Japanese in Asia. He had three forces in operation – the X-Force was a large Chinese force of Chinese an army of 15,000 or 20,000 Chinese soldiers that had been early in the war, taken to India, where they were trained, fed, and paid by the Americans. This was said to be very profitable for the Chinese Nationals. It took all the expense out of China itself and Stilwell always said, and was probably right, that if the Chinese soldier who had performed pretty badly in China itself, were properly trained, properly fed, and kept in good physical condition, that they would be just as good soldiers as the Japanese or the American, or even the Germans. A young group of the X-Forces stayed alongside of a famous American raid in Northern Burma in late 1943 or early 1944, Merril's Marauders. There was a movie made about that raid, the only battle of that kind that the Americans fought heavily in Burma, and alongside of them were the Chinese X-Forces that Stilwell had trained. They all had a terrible time of the jungle and reached the edge of Myitkyina, their pivotal point to fly to China but never managed to capture the city or the airfield before they had to withdraw. In the meantime, the Americans were building their road from Ledo, which was from southeast Assam and was to join the old Burma Road at Myitkyina. It would add another 150 to 200 miles for the trucks to travel to Kunming. The connection was finally made about May of 1945, and they found they couldn't carry a lot of supplies on the road because of road conditions and length. It took so much gasoline that they couldn't carry a lot and the initial attempts had the trucks carry so much fuel for themselves, that they could only carry about 700 pounds of cargo. Then the trucks were abandoned at Kunming or given to the Chinese because there wasn't enough gasoline to drive them back on the road. So it was really a one-way road.

As I mentioned earlier, the original trucks were old and I had two of them to start with, which makes two drivers and two helpers to keep them running, and then got a third one after a couple of weeks – about May of 1944. The trucks were in very bad shape, but the drivers were helpful. My original loaders were hired Chinese coolies. Americans, by the way, (I guess everybody does) always name other people something. The Chinese were en masse, known as "slopies." There were "limies" (British), and we once called the Germans the "huns," and so forth. Coolies or slopies is not a very good name, I guess, but you have to have something to talk about.

After about two months of handling the freight, I was told Stilwell's Y-Force was to train the Chinese and build a Chinese army in Yunan Province to approach Burma from the Chinese side, to fight the Japanese in Myitkina and so that area would be hit from both their east and north side, along with opening up the road to China again. His Y-Force was in existence and was training some Chinese Nationalist troops around Kunming and a couple of other towns towards Burma. They were Yunanni and Paoshan, the last two towns in China before you hit the Burmese border. The Y-Force was training 2,000 Chinese by the time I got there. The Z-Force, the one I was originally assigned to was to train Chinese to fight in the South China coast where everyone assumed the American Army would be landing. Fortunately, this never had to be done.

The whole theater, the CBI (China, Burma, India), which was not too well thought of by the powers in the world, was the end of the line. When I was in India, Lord Louis Mountbatten, from England, was appointed as the supreme commander of the CBI, just like Eisenhower was the supreme commander of the ETO. Lord Mountbatten set up headquarters in a lovely spot, the capital of Ceylon, Kandy. It was supposed to be a resort area and Ceylon was full of English tea planters and high society types. His troops, not in an affectionate way, usually referred to him as Lord Louis Noncombatant, the reason being that there was great disappointment in the English in India, that there was never any major English plan or attempt of any kind to retake Rangoon and Burma. There was no talk of a second front in Burma, so Lord Louis Noncombatant was well known in the area. I saw him just once, when he flew into Kunming in a big British bomber of some sort, to have a conference with General Chennault. Naturally, I was not included in the conference, but I did see him get out of his airplane.

Speaking of politics, here's another example of it. A good deal of the war in China, the parts I saw, and this is pretty much common knowledge, I think, and even though I was on the sidelines, listening to anyone who had any knowledge. China was divided into at least three parts, one was the Chinese Nationalists, and their armies with Chiang Kai-shek as the Generalissimo, and was as much a dictator in China as Adolph in Germany. The Americans were divided into two groups, the American Air Force, under General Chennault and the American ground forces, under General Joseph Stilwell. There was competition between Stilwell and Chennault for the supplies. The agreements that came out of the Cairo meetings of the heads of state, which included Stalin, Roosevelt, and Churchill, was that the Air Force was to get the primary support in China and Stilwell got what the Air Force didn't need and could be flown in. The Air Force got the first five or ten thousand tons that were flown over the hump every month, so they got the cream of the crop in the beginning, and later flights. The Air Force still got over half, maybe three-fourths of what was flown in. A good deal of what was called hump tonnage was simply gasoline to fly all the airplanes, and much of the gasoline was brought in modified B-24 bombers, called C-109s, which was a tanker version. The gasoline for the ground forces came in the unsafe way of 55-gallon drums, which sometimes leaked. We had a dump next to my warehouse, a field which we stored any that came in until we could deliver them. There was always a coating of gasoline and oil on the ground.

On top of the three major groups, in a sense, Nationalist Chinese, with armies of certainly several million men, General Chennault 14th Air Force and Joseph Stilwell, with the Y-Force and Z-Force that never got off the ground, competing for who was going to fight the best against the Japanese, the air or ground forces. The rest of China was Communistic. In addition, the Chinese province of Yunan had a warlord named Lung, who had an army of his own of a million men and they were quite distinguishable from the Chinese Nationalist Army. They were the local army of a Chinese warlord, and they all wore blue uniforms; the Chinese Nationalist Army, which came from all over China, but not too many from Yunan Province, wore a khaki uniform. You always knew which ones were which.

In 1944, the latter part of the summer, the disagreements between Chiang Kai-shek and General Stilwell came to a head. Stilwell said Chiang Kai-shek was not using what supplies we did give him to fight the Japanese, but were stockpiling what supplies, ammo, etc., that the Americans supplied to him for the coming battle with the Chinese Communists, which had an army of several million, some people said five million, in Northern China, who lived in caves in the northern part of the country. They were led by General Mao Tse-Tung. Had Stillwell been able to force a coalition to fight the Japanese of the Nationalists and the Communists ever taken place, it certainly would have been a different world. What happened though, because of his all popularity in the United States and with the U.S. Army, Chiang Kai-shek ended up as the winner of the battle of who got what and the support of the United States, which in the long run, was certainly a large mistake. It makes one wonder what would have happened, had it turned out the other way. The real result of this, which was bad, (certainly from my standpoint) somehow affected my job, was that this was when General Stilwell was recalled. The President sent General Pat Hurley over to China to Chunking to investigate and in the end, General Stilwell supported the ground troops and the Chinese in many ways. He spoke perfect Chinese, having spent years in the country during World War I and II, was recalled and was never allowed to set foot again in China, as part of his recall. He was, as I remember reading somewhere, present at the Japanese surrender in Tokyo Bay, but even then was not allowed to visit friends in China.

13. DAY BY DAY AT AIR FREIGHT

So, there I was in Kunming, China, with three trucks and some Chinese coolies, truck drivers from the old Burma road project, trying to see that the supplies for the ground forces were delivered to the right places and not stolen. All the roads and airfields were guarded by Chinese Nationalist troops, and one of the first things I started was that no truck with supplies for the ground forces could leave the exit by the beginning of the airport runway without a pass signed by me, F.B. Evans, and also a Chinese chop I was given, a stamp with my name in Chinese. This did not affect the Air Force; their complete installation of all kinds, warehouses, buildings for their personnel were all on the other side, the southeast side of the airport, and they never came through or had anything to do with the north side, where I was,. It was an interesting situation – each truck that left not only had to have the pass for the guard to get off the truck and out of the airport, but the person riding with the truck had to be sure that the loads were delivered. He had a ticket I wrote that said something like "two trucks loaded with gasoline or medical supplies" for whatever place they were going, medical depot for example, that had to be signed at the other end and returned to me. I started for a short time there with just myself and the truck, and I soon got a couple of helpers who stayed with me as long as I was there, through 1944 and to the end of the war and somewhat after, until I got away. These two people were also assigned to Z-Force, and like me, were put on temporary duty, which turned out to be permanent assignment in the air freight section. One of these ended up as a clerk in my office, the other one was a foreman, as I got more help.

In the late summer or fall of 1944, we finally got some American trucks to deliver the goods and my GI force grew to, at one time, in late 1944 and early 1945, to nine people assigned to simply ride in the trucks and supervise the loading. Of the two people that started with me, one became the office clerk because he could type; the other was sort of an overall watchdog and supervisor of the other GIs to make sure they were on the job, seven or more of them regularly. The Chinese army usually supplied a company of men to do the physical loading – a company being a couple of hundred Chinese soldiers. My main job was to watch over everything and tell everyone where to take things, and also to try to control, not only with the requirements of the tickets to get off the airfield, but the men accompanying the trucks to the depots, and to see that theft was kept to a minimum. I think it was fairly successful in that respect. I let everyone know in the air freight under me know that stealing by either the Chinese or Americans was not going to be tolerated in any sense. Most were very cooperative, although there were a few lapses where I looked the other way. Once in a while when we got some decent food shipped in from India, a case of canned peaches suddenly broke open, and I never said anything when the GIs handling them took some; all I said was no more than one can per man. Occasionally, there was loose clothing and people got an extra shirt, but there was no large amount taken at the airfield and no black marketing. There was absolutely no selling of anything to anybody. Things I had to watch most closely were medical supplies because even a small bottle was valuable and people said you could get up to perhaps $1,000.00 for a bottle of a hundred sulpha pills. That was American money, by the way, and not Chinese CN. One of the truckdrivers one day offered to make me a rich man when we got a shipment of gasoline in, but I didn't bite. Gasoline for the ground forces was always, at least in 1944, in very short supply. We got a couple of planeloads of gasoline, when the ground forces in Kunming were down to only two barrels. I suddenly had eighteen barrels, all flown in for us, they were offloaded near the warehouse. We then loaded them on two trucks to take them to the official gasoline dump. The driver wanted me to let him take the two truckloads of gasoline to town, and if I would agree to this before he left with the loads, he would bring me $18,000.00 American dollars, $1,000 per 55-gallon drum. I just laughed at him and told him to forget it. Gasoline was going to the gasoline depot, and I was personally escorting the two truckloads of them, so I missed my chance to get rich all at once. It didn't hurt my reputation with the troops who worked for me, though, they knew there wasn't going to be any black marketing of any kind.

In the late summer of 1944, the Chinese built a freight platform for our freight for the ground forces. It was a platform of truck height so that things did not have to get down to the ground in the warehouse. It was roughly three feet off the ground, about 40 feet wide, 140 feet long and roofed over. The only enclosed part of it was a small office at one end about 15 x 20 feet, which was my office headquarters. The person, who was one of the first to join me, was from up-state New York and about 33 years old; and as he could type; he became the 'office manager.' I'm not totally sure just exactly what he did; he spent a great deal of his time typing letters, and recommending his own promotion. He came in as a PFC and went out two years later the same way. He was, however, a very reliable person.

The other one was a younger man, from Brooklyn, New York and 27 years old; he was also very helpful.

In addition to them, I had a Chinese interpreter, who spoke the local Yunanese and other Chinese languages, Mr. Li, and he worked full time for me. For more than a year there, a Chinese refugee from Hong Kong who had been an executive in a Hong Kong travel agency and spoke perfect Cantonese, could read Chinese, was hired, with my approval, and did all kinds of things for us. His only problem was that he couldn't speak Yunanese; he could only speak it as well as I could which was about three or four words. The only Chinese words I can remember right now are three common words for the soldiers; one was Ding Hao – everything that was right in China was Ding Hao (good, okay, etc.); another was Gham-Bei, which was the equivalent of "cheers" when you had a drink; and the final one was JingBao, which was sort of an all-purpose word – air raids were called JingBaos, the gates that protected the old city and wall of Kunming were the JingBao gates so they reflected something of that kind of nature.

To revise an earlier statement and checking my notes, my air freight was the first major attempt in any war for a whole country to be supplied only by air. Maybe some of the things the Army learned through this was later expressed in the Berlin airlift, which was many times bigger than this one, but ours was the first major attempt to supply a country only by air when completely cut off.

On the black market theft side, I can only recall two instances of theft, one major and one I don't know how to rate. The major one was on a late Saturday, and I ended up with two trucks loaded with bales of clothing and nobody to escort them to the quartermaster depot, which was closing about then for the weekend, around 5 or 6 o'clock. So I left the trucks parked next to the loading platform. I went back to my tent like everyone else. When I showed up Monday morning, the trucks were gone. A couple of the GIs had gotten to work earlier than me so I immediately asked where the trucks were. Who delivered them? It turned out that nobody had. Somehow, over Sunday, someone had made off with two truckloads, each one with 60 bales of GI clothing on it were gone. I immediately called the military police and talked to them, with no satisfaction. They simply said tough luck (or t.s.), so I then called the CID, the investigation department of the army and finally got somebody there that seemed a little bit interested. He told me that if they were stolen on Sunday to forget it; they were already probably resold in Shanghai, so I lost not only the clothing but also the two trucks and nobody of importance in the army seemed to care.

The other item that mysteriously disappeared was that somewhere in late 1944, maybe December, somebody brought in a machine in a case to me and asked me where to send it. It was similar to a large typewriter case and I opened it up, as the key was hanging on a string attached to it. Inside was a machine somewhat like a typewriter, only it had two non-standard keyboards and a bunch of type rollers. It was obviously some kind of code machine; perhaps it was like an enigma machine that we later learned about. Anyway, nobody knew what to do with it; I called around and asked the personnel at the depots that I dealt with, like the quartermaster, I also called the MPs and the CID and anybody I could think of to see if anyone was interested in this very weird mechanical machine with two sets of keyboards. Nobody seemed to care a bit, so I brought the case in and put it under my desk, pushed up the chair, locked the office door and left. The following morning, when I got there everything seemed the same; the office was still locked; but the machine that I had carefully hid under my desk was gone. It was missing so I made calls to the CID, MPs, Theater Headquarters, and got no satisfaction or interest from anyone. Also, nobody that worked for me had any ideas or thoughts – they had forgotten about it. Whoever wanted it made off with it and that's all I can say, but he was certainly a clever thief. This was only one of the two major thefts that I recall.

My loading depot, which was much handier than the warehouse system, certainly helped speed things up, as the freight tonnage was steadily increasing. (A correction about an earlier remark of mine: checking the records and the letters – at the maximum in early 1945 and until the end of the war, I had a total of fifteen American GIs working for me, the two old-timers and thirteen others, who escorted the trucks). You were lucky if you could get them to take –two trucks – one they rode in and one that followed or vice versa, to a depot, one trip in the morning and one in the afternoon. I figure we got 26 deliveries a day, six days a week. There were thirteen GIs doing that and two in the office and the Chinese Government supplied interpreter, and the former travel agent executive from Hong Kong, who could read Chinese and was a very nice person, who did all kinds of odd jobs. He could communicate better than I could to the interpreter, who then instructed the Chinese coolies. The number of Chinese army assigned to load the loads averaged about 150 per day, a company of Chinese – some days 100 of them, other days there would be 200. Maybe some of them "went over the hill." They worked and did whatever they were told.

I did one thing for their benefit which didn't make me too popular with some people. I noticed very early that the Chinese officers did not treat their privates, or average soldiers very well. When they didn't do anything they wanted or as quickly as they wanted, they beat them with long bamboo poles (about 3 or 4 feet long). They beat them all over with this stick and kicked them to get them to do things faster. Through the interpreter, I sent the message that the American Army did not allow American soldiers or soldiers of any kind to be physically punished or beaten in any way. Some of the beatings stopped pretty quickly then, but not all of them. About three or four days later, I told the interpreter to get hold of those Chinese officers and to tell them that if the beatings of their own troops was not stopped immediately, I was going to hold a court martial and have those Chinese officers shot at sunrise. They had a long, somewhat screaming confrontation with the officers in charge of the Chinese company but from that day on, I never saw one of our Chinese soldiers hit with the bamboo sticks. So I did that much for them and I hope it spread somewhere else.

The GIs I had working for me were an assorted crew, some of them were fairly reliable, others did seem a bit prejudiced, but the younger ones we got later, eighteen year old draftees were hard to get to do anything, but they would escort the trucks when they were forced to. It seemed to me that the older the people were, the more responsible they were. I had some that were even in their late 30's that were assigned to me different times. There was some turnover in them but the maximum number totaled 15 GIs, 2 Chinese interpreters, and 150 Chinese soldiers, more or less working for me.

The job would have been much easier had there been any cooperation from the Air Force. I suspect that this came from the top from when Stilwell was still competing with Chennault for supplies over the Hump. When the planes landed, the Air Force sent their own trucks (many of them GI trucks that had been shipped over in parts and then welded back together) to unload the planes; theoretically with the crew chief of the cargo plane seeing that things were handled properly. They loaded the supplies for ground forces on their trucks and then dumped them on our loading platform. I tried several times to talk to the Air Force people at the operations where the Air Force manifests were handled, to having the unloading done directly onto our trucks, then so many of the loads would not have to be handled twice. After much screaming on my part, I guess word got out up the line but the only answer I got back was that the Air Force did it the Air Force way. I couldn't do anything except when they were through unloading and dumping the stuff on our platform, I could sign the Air Force manifest that we had received the goods, so that their paperwork was completely taken care of. Every plane had a manifest that took a page or two of listing items as the planes were loaded in India. There was, of course, no way that I could check the manifest against the stuff that showed up on our platform, except to look at the stuff and say, yes, that's medical supplies, etc. So, I ended up essentially signing for every manifest for every single item delivered to the Y-Forces and later to the Army Services of Supply and unless my signature was on the manifest, the Air Force wouldn't release it. A lot of people saw my signature, although I was pretty confident that they couldn't make me pay for how many millions of dollars worth of stuff came through. The Air Force did it their own way and there was nothing I could do about it. It would have cut down on labor by at least half, if not two-thirds, had the Air Force agreed to unload the planes right on the trucks that would deliver to the SOS warehouses.

One minor note the warehouse brings back to me. I did it one time when we were still in the warehouse where the platform storage was built. We received a couple of motorcycles, big Harleys for the MPs. I called the MPs and they said they'd pick them up when they got around to it. I noticed that the motorcycles had been used; in fact, they had full gas tanks, and were irresistible to me. I rode one around the warehouse area the better part of a day. The Chinese coolies always congregated in the warehouse so when I came in (the warehouse had two large doors, one at each side of the front of it – big enough for a truck to come in and out) they would stand in front of the door and wait until I got there and when I threw it in neutral, they would scatter, laughing and having lots of fun. I would go in one door and out the other and then come back. We spent the better part of the afternoon that way; after doing it several times, I got a little bolder and rode it faster. Then I didn't make the turn to leave and ran smack dab head-long into the wall and went over the front of the motorcycle. I thought I was going to come up with a high-pitched voice; I was bruised and had minor cuts, nothing that amounted to anything. I recovered and went to work the next day. There wasn't enough damage to go to the dispensary, but I never rode a motorcycle in China again. I just pushed them both up against the wall and called the MPs again and told them to come get their g.d. motorcycles before I gave them to someone else. And they did. Sometimes you get into funny situations, even when the general atmosphere is not what you would call fun.

Among the interesting sights in the airfield was the runway, (which I mentioned before how it was built by hand). The main runway ran diagonally across the airfield from the northeast end to the southwest. I guess this was due to the way the winds were usually coming from the west. All planes landed and took off always in the same direction. The beginning of the runway was roughly 100 yards from where my office was located on the loading platform. Before the beginning of the runway was an abandoned and pretty well fallen down small Chinese village, and from there the runway stretched 4,000 feet in the beginning. All planes seemed to land (touch down) at about the same spot, although there were planes bring freight from India and few fighter planes and bombers that were stationed there. The 14th Air Force often had some fighters coming in and many of them were photographic planes. I saw only one Lockheed P-38 taking off and landing, and this was written up in the local Army paper. We looked forward to this paper, the <u>CBI Roundup</u>, which had correspondents in India and China. A good deal of it was material from the 14th Air Force. A famous Michigan football player, Tom Harman, who was in the Air Force, came with his photographic plane and flew a lot of missions down to the China coast and to Hong Kong. He would be taking high-altitude photographs. Most of the military war planes were P-40 fighters and towards the very end of the war, some P-47s with large radial engines, heavy and quite fast, about 400 mph planes and could carry at least a 500 pound bomb. I would see them take off with a 500 pound bomb under them, so heavy, the tires were flat on the bottom, but pilots managed to get them in the air. The bombers we saw were two-engine B-25s, B-26s, and occasionally B-24s, which had four engines. That was the armament of the 14th Air Force that I saw.

One interesting plane that I saw several times was a B-26 bomber, that was not painted, but shiny aluminum. It was flown by Colonel Phil Cochran, who had been known for flying in Burma. He was one of the top people in General Chennault's command. He had his personal B-26 for getting around all the airfields. According to Air Force personnel, it was a souped-up version and had no armament, as it wasn't for fighting, just flying. Occasionally, I saw it happen this way maybe a dozen times at least, Cochran would pull this B-26 up to the very beginning of the runway and rev up the engines to maximum rpm. He would then release the brakes and start like a 'bat out of hell' down the runway. When he got about halfway down the runway, he pulled up the wheels, but the plane stayed at exactly the same level, maybe 8 or 10 feet above the runway. He stayed at that level until he came to the end of the runway, and then he would pull the stick back and zoom straight up into the air. He really put on a show.

To the southwest of the airport, there was a large mountain with a sheer-sided cliff that went up maybe 2,000 to 3,000 feet above the land. It was about 5 miles across Kunming Lake. If it had a name, I don't know what it was – everybody called it 'Red Mountain' because when the sun came up and (unfortunately we were usually all up) the sun shone on this bare cliff, it was red. It was beautiful; there were also snow-capped peaks in the distance. The bad part I remember about it was that one day I watched a Chinese Air Force P-40 take off rather slowly, gain altitude over the lake, and smash head-on into Red Mountain.

I watched the explosion and said a short prayer for the pilot. That's part of being on an airfield during a war.

I saw one other major accident which I wish I hadn't. A B-24, apparently loaded with ammunition and bombs for a mission, started rather slowly down the runway from where I could see it. By the time it got near the end of the runway, it still didn't look like it was going to get in the air. As I watched, it was trying to get airborne, and didn't; it simply plowed on past the end of the runway. I grabbed a couple of my people, jumped into my jeep and headed down the runway to see if we could do anything. By the time we got near the end of the runway, perhaps a few seconds later, it was just a mass of fire, exploding ammunition and the bombs went off. Unfortunately, a report came back, stating there were 11 GIs aboard, including pilot, co-pilot, crew chiefs, gunners, etc. It was a horrible sight to see.

Kunming had two different periods in the war, when I was there, which were considered war zones. We were within approximately 100 miles from the closest Japanese army. There was pretty good protection on both sides but it was considered an active theater of the war. That is why I was twice given battle stars to wear on the Asiatic Pacific Ribbon. In my time, we had only three air raids in Kunming when Japanese bombers came over. We had one or two in 1944, and one in 1945. The last one, in 1945, was to me, somewhat interesting in that apparently everybody knew it was going to happen early in the evening when the mountains around Kunming suddenly had a lot of fires, obviously lit by Japanese sympathizers to guide the bombers from east to west and across the north. Bonfires were set about every mile or so. Sure enough, around 10:00 that night, twenty-four Japanese bombers appeared. The sirens had gone off and I was in a slit trench, trying to sleep, using my helmet for a pillow when I heard the planes. I looked up and saw the planes about 1,000 or more feet above me so I shouldered my trusty carbine and took a shot, my one shot at the enemy in the war. A chance of my hitting a Japanese airplane in that situation was about one in 100 million and if it hit it, there was another chance of one in a billion that it would have done any damage. At least I got my one shot off though. The planes flew over the airport and dropped bombs, mostly in the parking area, small fragmentation bombs; they did a little damage, but not much. Any holes were filled in by the next morning. I walked around the area where the bombs were dropped, picked up a couple of pieces of fragmentation that had exploded, and the tail fins from a small five-pound bomb. I carted these around for twenty-five years, and finally got sick of them; nobody had any interest in them so finally, in one of the moves in Florida, I simply tossed them out. At this point, they would make an interesting picture for this story of mine, but I don't think I have any pictures of them, but if I find one, I'll add it. I carted them around in my barracks bag all over China and back to this country and through a dozen moves in the United States, and then threw them in the wastebasket.

Now, to get back to Colonel Cochran's handling of an airplane, which was certainly spectacular. He became famous – he was picked up by an extremely popular comic strip in the United States, <u>Terry and the Pirates</u>. It was the number one comic strip and his name was changed to Flip Corkin and it certainly pleased a lot of people and ran for several years. You could look it up in any old newspaper because the comic strip was carried in almost every newspaper in the United States. One of the other characters in the comic strip that was famous was the Dragon Lady, and this was the name often applied to Madame Soong, Generalissimo's wife, one of the famous Soong sisters, the one who was a close friend of Roosevelt and stayed at the White house.

This recalls to mind an incident in June or July of 1944. Madame Soong had been in Washington, staying at the White House, entertaining people, and was quite popular in the United States. She had a lot of political influence, not only with the President but with all kinds of Washington people. She came back on her own airplane, all the way by air from Washington to Miami, to Brazil, Africa, Cairo, India, and over the Hump on CNAC. She had two DC-3 airplanes that she came with, and according to one of the CNAC pilots that I knew, she came with some of her entourage and Chinese friends in one, and the second DC-3 belonged to CNAC, of which she was the major owner, contained her luggage. Her luggage consisted of sixteen large steamer trunks, which were said to be filled with everything from money to fancy clothing and cosmetics. She also had twenty-four wooden cases of Coca Cola, old style wooden case which covered only about 40% of the bottle. The steamer trunks were about three feet square and four or five feet high and they were brought to the warehouse, along with the Coca Cola. Some of the loading people didn't think much of Madame Soong, and they had no way of showing it, but they did manage to drop some of her trunks off the forklifts as they picked them up off the ground. There's no telling what the contents were like when the trunks were opened. Two large Mongolian looking guards, ferocious six-footers were posted with the trunks and the Coca Cola so that nobody could snitch even a single bottle. Later, everything was loaded on a CNAC plane, and taken to

Chunking. I never did see Madame Soong, the Dragon Lady, but I often wondered what kind of shape the things in her trunk were after being dropped about 15 feet onto concrete.

The planes that brought the supplies over the Hump flew through pretty bad weather and after General Tunner took over, they flew around the clock, no more daylight only. They lost quite a few planes. It started out completely with C-47 (DC-3s), which could carry only 3,500 pounds maximum to get the altitude to get over the Hump. Starting in the Summer of 1944, the Air Force switched to C-46 Curtis Commandos, two-engines, originally three bladed props, later models four-bladed, radial engines of 1,000 horsepower each. They could carry up to four tons, more than twice what a C-46 carried. The biggest thing you could get into a C-47 was a jeep; a stripped down "weapons carrier" could fit easily into the Curtis Commando. The military designation of these Curtis Commando planes was C-46 and how they got a lower number than the C-47 DC-3s I don't know. As far as I know, they were never used commercially. One thing I did know was that before they turned around to go back to India for more supplies, every one of them was loaded with 200 pounds of ingots of pure tin from a local foundry towards the tail of the plane, as far back in the cargo compartment as possible. This was required to balance the plane so that it could properly take off and fly "empty". I often wondered what they did with all those ingots of tin in Upper Assam, probably a big pile of them in the jungle somewhere still there. Who knows?

Occasionally, and quite rarely, we got a DC-4 (C-54), with four engines, and carried a bit more than the Curtis Commando plane. Two versions of the B-24 four-motor bomber were used, mostly by the Air Force. One was simply used for cargo and was designated a C-87, I think, and then a tanker version, large tanks that had to be emptied when it got to Kunming, was called a C-109. These were the planes that brought everything the Americans paid for to China. I never did see a jet in China; I don't know if any ever got into combat in Europe or not; I know the Germans had some by then. Anyway, the planes flew over the Hump day and night through the world's worst weather and the estimated loss of planes was very high. This means the minimum of 500 to 1000 crew members were lost. One of the common stories was that the tallest mountain they flew over, Mount Tally, 22,000 feet, was known as the first mountain wrapped in aluminum, from the wrecks on it. And we handled what they brought us the best we could.

The best estimates that I recall were that in the approximately four years of flying supplies into China, of all kinds, from the United States, about a million tons were flown to China from India. Of these million tons, if that's a fair estimate, three quarters of them probably went through Kunming, since it was the main base. Very few flights flew direct to any other fields.

At one time in 1944, the ATC said they were going to set a record in one day of a hundred airplanes of freight to Kunming and they made it. When that day came, it was like August 1, or something that was to be our 100 ton day. The way they made the 100 tons, there were no flights for about three days before that so all the planes were lined up in India, waiting to all go on the same day. They then set a record of 100 airplanes to Kunming that one day. I never tried to count the total traffic, but I would imagine in eight hours on an average day, there were probably 300 to 400 take offs and landings, including all kinds of military planes, down to an occasional L-5 Taylor Cub, and the small

Chinese Air Force who flew P-40s. At one time, a two-person helicopter showed up and flew around the airport for a week or so. After several days of flying around, it crashed about a half a mile down the road from where my office was. I never saw another helicopter until much later, back in this country.

The Hump losses were over a hundred airplanes, so it was a major effort of the United States to have that many planes fly in all kinds of conditions. Of the millions of tons of freight shipped to China over the Hump during four years of war, more than two-thirds, if not 80% of them, went to the Air Corps. A lot that being gasoline for their own uses, and the things I handled were a variety of whatever the Army needed, from food (not as much of it as I wish or the right kind), clothing, gasoline, engineering supplies, ammunition, medical supplies of all kinds, and personnel being transferred to China (of course, they didn't go through the warehouse), but we did sort them all out and try to send cargo to the right place, with some success, I think. It was certainly the first time an air support had really worked. The story, they may be blowing up their own importance, but in 1945, the Air Force claimed the airport at Kunming was the busiest airport in the world. In terms of losses, we didn't get too many reports or the people in operations didn't want to talk about them, but there was one night in January 1945 of terrible storms. The operations people told me that in that one night of bad storms, they lost 15 airplanes which went down over the Hump. The reason I got the information about them was about a week later, when I made my daily trip to this operations to sign the manifests so they would turn the cargo loose to us, I found a bunch of manifests for items that I thought I had never seen. The people in operations then admitted that these half dozen manifests were copies from the planes that went down and they wanted them signed as being received because they didn't want the records to simply show that those planes never reached their destinations. I simply refused to sign the manifests because they were for supplies we had never received. So I told them where they could put their manifests. I never signed for things that I knew we had not received. On the other hand, we sometimes got load after load of things I didn't know what in the world they were going to do with. For maybe a month half the loads we got contained 2 ½ and 3" pipe in 20' lengths, iron pipe, literally thousands of them in a month's time. Each piece of pipe weighed about one hundred pounds. Anyway, we sent them all to the engineers. The story was that the Chinese were going to take them and build a gasoline pipeline to connect down the Burma Road so that when the Lido Road opened and the stuff was flowing in, they could meet them at the Chinese border with gasoline. I never saw any construction being started for a pipeline along the Chinese end of the Burma Road. I have a picture, if I can ever find it, of a rock with "1" carved on it which was the start, mile one of the Burma Road just outside Kunming.

Among other items I got literally hundreds of were water purification machines. These were crated machines that had a small gasoline engine, some machinery of other kind that I couldn't tell you what it was, and a wooden tank that held 100 or more gallons. These were all on a skid and marked water purification for the engineers. It seemed that on every flight we had one or more of these. They were to be used to purify the water for drinking when the big American landing in the South Coast of China took place. These water purifying machines would then be available so that the Americans wouldn't have to drink the water out of the rivers. There must have been more than 1,500 of them stacked up in the engineering compound area before they stopped sending them.

Occasionally, we got a few PX supplies that came through, but never enough it seemed, of the right things. One of the letters I saved to my father mentioned that I had gotten my PX rations for the month: one carton of cigarettes at a cost of 40 cents (no taxes and no freight) for a carton of Lucky Strikes and two La Palina cigars, and if you wanted, a bag of Bull Durm tobacco with papers attached, and a couple of candy bars. That was a typical ration. I think one month we got three cartons of cigarettes, which really made our smokers, like me, happy; fortunately out of my crews, there was always one or two who didn't smoke and didn't want them and they knew the best thing they could do was sell them to me. I always paid them $1.00 for their carton or sometimes when we got a couple of Hershey bars, I traded them – a candy bar for a pack of cigarettes. I managed to smoke my daily quota of sometimes a pack a day and other times a lot less, maybe two or three because I had run out. We sure didn't get much from the PX, a lot of hard candy that nobody seemed to want and some chocolates occasionally that were made for the tropics – they did everything except taste like chocolate. We got other things too, sometimes food on holidays, around Thanksgiving we got lots of canned turkey, which was really pretty good. It came in quart-sized cans and again the same kind of thing at Christmas. I don't remember any chicken coming through. One thing we did get a lot of that made me sick (as well as a lot of other people), was corned beef, and according to the markings on the box, it was canned in Paraguay and Uruguay, South America in 1917, apparently to be shipped to the American Army in Europe in

WWI. Instead, it ended up in a warehouse somewhere in the United States, and somebody said we have to get rid of that stuff, it's getting old, it was already twenty-five years old in the cans; and about half of the cans were rancid and green inside. But the mess halls managed to serve a lot of it. I couldn't eat it at all. We got a lot of odds and ends like that, the Army was cleaning out warehouses and whenever they didn't know what to do, they would just send it to China. We got hundreds of 1903 Springfield rifles for the Chinese, they shot the 30.06 cartridge, common in our Army but not in the Chinese army. These were brand new, packed in grease, called cosmoline; we also got some Thompson submachine guns, the old type with a round drum to fill with 45s. I often pitied the poor Chinese that had to get all that grease off them before they could use them – if they ever did. It was obviously a warehouse clearing operation. We also got ammunition and occasionally bombs. Often, there were people in the factories who would sign with women's names, like Sally and so forth, and would have messages on them in chalk or crayon; it usually read something like, "shove this one up a Jap's ass," and other clever remarks like that.

I have no idea how many Americans died in China, the Air Force probably has an accurate count of their own people, but of the ground forces, I have no idea. I do know there was a cemetery set up for Americans in Kunming. They were buried in graves like the Chinese, above ground because of knowing that when the monsoons came, the ground would be so saturated that any coffin in the ground would float away. The tombs of the Chinese and Americans were all above ground, they were fired brick and the shape of a half cylinder, curved top so that water could roll off, and with two straight ends. After a coffin was put in it, it was bricked up. The last time I passed the cemetery, which I did often on my way to various places, there were probably at least 100 American tombs. I talked, at different times, to some of the people that worked in graves registration; we called them bad names, such as 'ghoul', because they buried the dead. The only different thing I can remember about them was that one explained to me that there were two things that had to be done whenever an American died over there. One was that someone, either the grave registration people or the people he lived with had to go through everything that the person had in belongings, including what he had on him. His personal things had to be sorted through for things that needed to be sent to the family, usually letters, photos, and money. The graves registration people took the bodies to the cemetery, put them in a casket and removed the shoes and clothing. The reason they removed the shoes was that in the beginning, people were known to rob the above-ground graves and steal the shoes and sometimes the clothing. After the first few times, it was learned how valuable the shoes were on the black market. Since word got around fairly quickly, most of the bodies thereafter were buried without clothing and especially without shoes. Fortunately, that was my only experience dealing with the graves registration people. I do not recall that we shipped any bodies anywhere nor did we receive any to bury there.

14. PILOTS

I didn't know the pilots of the planes because those who brought all the freight were Air Force and went to the Air Force side of the field. But with operations next door to where I worked, I did see a few, including one who was a well-known CNAC pilot who had come over with Pan American originally, and apparently had a family in China (although he was an American), of Italian descent. His last name was Monju; he had a brother who was a very well-known character actor in Hollywood. He regularly flew the route from Calcutta all the way to Chunking, stopping in Kunming, and talked to anybody who would listen, like me. I saw him off and on for the first four or five months that I was on the field. He then disappeared – the Air Force people talked to the CNAC people, and said he had crashed somewhere between Kunming and Chunking. He lived through the crash, and was in the hospital, and would be going home soon. He probably did, as I never saw him again.

The other is a famous group of pilots, the American Volunteer Group (AVG), later known and famous as the Flying Tigers. There was one flying tiger pilot left when I got there. The Flying Tigers had been formed in 1941, and they were under the control of General Chennault, who was then head of the Chinese Air Force. They were pure mercenaries, hired in the United States, volunteers to come fly P-40s, of which there were about 50 in Rangoon, waiting to be used. They were hired to come fly those against the Japanese. They were to be paid, initially $1,000 a month, and later raised to $1,500, and given a bonus of $500 for each Japanese plane they shot down.

The immediate need was that the Japanese for some time had been regularly bombing Kunming, on an almost daily basis. The AVG was designed to try and stop that bombing, and the way it turned out, they did. The person who told me all these stories was a pilot, who had not gone home yet – apparently he had a family and children in Kunming, and household belongings, so he was hanging around every day for these six weeks that I talked to him. He was trying to wangle himself, his family, and his furniture free ride from out of Calcutta, which I assume he finally did get organized. He had a lot of stories about the AVG. He was in the last group.

The Flying Tigers were not just one group of pilots – their initial group was maybe 25 pilots and they were they purely there for the money. In those days, they could make as much money in a year as the President of the United States. Their $1,000 a month matched what a lot of heads of companies made so they were making that much and then more with their bonuses. Not only were they pilots, they were also mechanics and other personnel to keep the planes flying. Essentially, they were quartered in Rangoon, which was a pleasant place to be; it was on the Gulf of Bengal or the river that ran into it. It was surrounded by English tea plantations with a lot of English society that immediately adopted these young American pilots. This was even before Pearl Harbor. They got to party and go to the English country club.

When they were on a mission, they flew from Rangoon to Kunming, where they refueled and sometimes picked up ammunition for their machine guns. They weren't equipped for any bombing, but they did have six or eight machine guns mounted in the wings. He said that General Chennault developed the tactic that they used, which was to fly as high as they could get these P-40s over Kunming, and when Japanese planes came into view, they dove on them as fast as they could, making one pass, firing their machine guns. After making the one pass, they were out of gas and headed back for Kunming Airfield. This was the technique they used because the plane wasn't very good, but was easy to fly and very strong and it could absorb a lot of punishment. It could dive much faster than any Zero, because the Zeroes weren't heavy enough and would fall apart. This same technique was later used by a successful marine in the South Pacific, and the person who took this technique to the South Pacific was a famous marine pilot, Greg Boyington, Pappy Boyington of the Black Sheep Squadron, which had a television show made about it. The AVG was where Boyington started as a pilot. The pilots had a good time flying in China because they were making so much money. Most of them came in on a six-month contract, so it was twenty-five different pilots every six months for about two years. They primarily thought of themselves primarily as the American Volunteer Group, and always referred to it as the AVG. General Chennault denied that it was part of the American Air Force but it later came out that it really was a part of our Air Force, only treated differently in many ways. The living in Rangoon was great; there were plenty of gorgeous English and Burmese girls around and they partied all the time. In 1942, shortly after Pearl Harbor, and the Japanese were invading Burma, the AVG was disbanded. Chennault gathered all the pilots together in Kunming and offered them all direct commissions as second lieutenants in the American Army Air Force, and they all started laughing, as a second lieutenant in the Air Force made $125 to $135 a month, so they laughed and said "no thank you." Only two said they would stay and join the American Air Force. The rest of them said they were going home. They didn't quit flying immediately on the day they told Chennault they were through; they still flew into Kunming, flying in everything they could buy and put in the cockpit in Rangoon, and resell in Kunming. They carried mostly cosmetics, but occasionally they got gold from the banks – anything they could buy in Rangoon was worth anywhere from two to ten times what they paid for it in Kunming in American money. The pilot who told me these stories said he took out the radio so he could put more lipsticks in the cockpit with him, because there wasn't any storage space. They made a lot of money to take home with them, which at least proves that they were indeed good mercenaries. They didn't look at all like John Wayne did in the movie *Flying Tigers*, but they were successfully enough shooting down Japanese bombers, that the Japanese stopped the daily regular bombing of Kunming and didn't resume them.

As I indicated earlier, I think we had only three air raids in my close to three years in Kunming. The one thing that was missing, and they should have had it in the John Wayne movie, was the wooden shack of operations, with a sign that said "Kunming, China, altitude 6,240 feet."

15. <u>KUNMING LIFE</u>

Kunming was not much of a city to visit and often I didn't bother to go on weekends. The only reason to go there was to get something to drink, but I had cut my drinking down to just Saturday night. Too many people had gotten in the habit of drinking every day and every night and every morning to get started and essentially turned into drunks. One of these people I knew, was a lawyer, who was a very fine person, but who eventually ended up a hopeless alcoholic.

Kunming, as a city, was filthy (that's a nice word for it), with dirt everywhere, including the stores and restaurants. In the mornings, buckets with night soil were out to be picked up. The people were relatively friendly. One of the things that always surprised me was that not only were American cigarettes popular, but cigarette butts also were. You threw away a cigarette – the Chinese would scramble to pick it up, still burning, and they would puff on it. They also ended up great cigarette makers. Merchants would sit on the street with a box of cigarette butts and shred them for the tobacco in them, and then roll new cigarettes out of them. Sometimes I would feel sorry for them and throw down a cigarette I had just lit so they could have a fairly decent smoke.

The city had been bombed and a lot of buildings had been severely damaged and everywhere you went there were rats, including the three different hospitals. The rats in China were like rats I had never seen before. These were rats probably close to two feet long, bigger than most cats. The only way you could kill them was with a 45 automatic weapon. You couldn't kill them with a broom stick; they were very aggressive and they would challenge you if you cornered them.

Kunming also had a little river running through it – it wasn't a very big river. You could stop on a bridge over it and watch and within 50 yards of the bridge there would be women washing clothes, men and women washing themselves, people washing their potatoes, cabbages, and food, and other people dumping garbage, such as night soil all into the same river.

There were a good many elderly women of all classes, from the very lowest to those that were well-dressed and riding in rickshaws. These women were probably fifty years old and older, who had their feet bound, which was a Chinese custom, when they were babies. These women had feet perhaps three to four inches long. The amazing thing to me was wondering about the terrible pain it must have caused them when they were bound and how well they could get around. They took very short steps, but they could run like mad. I was surprised to see customs like that in a country we couldn't imagine how backward parts of it were, especially the inner lands. The Yunan Province, to some people was like Texas in the United States, which I don't think was a compliment to either of them.

In early 1945, I had another attack of bad stomach problems and dysentery, one of the worst attacks I had ever had. I went to sick call and got examined by an MD on duty and he poked me a few times and heard me scream, and decided I had appendicitis. I was taken to the American hospital about twenty miles away, it was a pretty good sized hospital, with about 200 beds, six or seven wards, with 30 people in each ward. He put a red tag on me, marked appendix, and called for an ambulance. The ambulance came within an hour, and gave me the bumpiest ride I had ever had. By the time I got to the hospital, I was about ready to give up everything. I went into the waiting room and found a bench where I lay down and then passed out. The next thing I knew, I was awakened by a GI with a broom, who was sweeping the place out. I had been laying there from noon until nine o'clock that night. He came over and shook me to make sure I was alive. He saw the tag and went off to find a doctor. The doctor decided I didn't have appendicitis, but that I had malaria, so he put me in a malaria ward, along with 29 other people. I got a soft diet and a lot of tea to drink. Twice a day, they sampled my blood to determine the type of malaria I had to start malaria treatment. Some of the medicine turned the whites of your eyes to yellow, but it was used to prevent malaria. I lasted through it, and I still have my appendix. The only other occurrence in the hospital was one that kept me mad for a long time, years to be truthful. About the second or third day I was there, a Red Cross lady came through with a basket full of candy and cigarettes. I immediately asked for some cigarettes. She demanded thirty cents and told me I couldn't have the cigarettes if I didn't pay for them. I told her we bought them in the PX for forty cents a carton, and on hers where the tax stamp usually is, it said "donated by union local such and such, Detroit, Michigan." So, they were donated free and here was this Red Cross worker selling them for thirty cents a pack. She told me if I didn't like it, I didn't have to buy them, but that's the way it was. It took me a long time to get over that – she was also selling chocolate candy for 10 cents when we could get them elsewhere for 3 cents. After about 8 or 9 days in the malaria ward, I screamed loud enough that they released me and I went back to my regular job. I was welcomed back by some of the people and others, I expect would have been happier had I never come back.

After one other attack, I went to the dispensary in a different area, and the doctor said he could cure me of my dysentery. He filled a large water glass full of paregoric; I knew what it was, only by the occasional teaspoons I had taken before. He poured me a nine ounce glass of it and told me to drink it down and I did. I stopped to go to the latrine and came back to the dispensary. I knew what opium was and had seen some become addicted to it. So, for the next twenty-four hours or more I was walking in one of the big cirrus cumulous clouds up above. Each step I took I was walking in the clouds, floating in air and I never felt better in my life, and how I got back to my own area and tent, I don't know but I did. It also made me understand how the elderly Chinese felt – there were many opium dens in Kunming with old men with opium pipes, which were bamboo pipes and had small brass bowls at the end. The attendant would come by and fill the bowls and light the pipes for them. The men would then pay for the opium. These opium dens were nothing like what you see in the movies, they were dirty rooms with double-decked wood beds and that was about the extent of it. I never did try to smoke it, but I did purchase an opium pipe as a souvenir. I have no idea what I did with the pipe, probably traded it with somebody for a couple of cigarettes.

I kept my stomach problems pretty much under control mainly by not eating. There was a lot of food served in our mess hall, and most of it was local-raised products. Not many of the cooks were Chinese. Much of our food was water buffalo, as slaughtered and eaten by the Chinese too. I found it fairly edible, but it was tough. We had fresh eggs when they were available, otherwise powdered eggs, served every morning. They didn't taste like much, and were sandy in taste. We had spam – a good treat, fried spam. Another was, affectionately known in the Army, as SOS, (shit on a shingle), which is fried ground beef in cream sauce and actually, it was fairly edible. By not eating much, and usually only twice a day, I managed to lose a lot of weight.

In mid-1945, my weight was down below 100 pounds, which was about 50 pounds less than I weighed when I went into the army and I looked pretty scrawny. I made a mistake and sent a picture of me to Bobbie with no shirt on and she got quite upset. I didn't send any more pictures after that. She was very good about writing, usually about twice a week and I answered one. I also wrote to my father and grandfather. There was so much boredom there and no activities. The movies we got were so old, I didn't bother to go to them. There were no organized sporting events. We didn't have any softball or basketball games either. Other than combat fighting, boredom is the worst thing in the army.

The things you missed the most, avoiding some of the obvious, in Kunming, and the things most talked about when people were always looking for more were, first, letters from home; second was toilet paper, which was in great shortage; and third, cigarettes. Companionship was somewhere way below any of those items as far as immediate needs went. I guess number four on my list would be drink, and I knew hardly anybody who didn't drink while we were there. I probably drank more than I should have on Saturday nights, but it was cheap. In the little bar down the road from where I lived, they often, when you bought a bottle for $1.50, would put a little plate of peanuts on the table for you. I learned how to use chopsticks by picking up the peanuts one at a time. I can still eat an entire Chinese meal with chopsticks from all that practicing although I never did learn to eat the rice the way the Chinese did. It looked like almost shoveling it in your mouth.

Another experience I remember well and had some notes on was about once a month I had to go to nearby airfields. There were two within about twenty miles of Kunming and occasionally a plane destined for Kunming ended there by mistake and I would have to go there to check on the supplies. I went to a small town about thirty miles away to a village near the airfield that was walled and had wooden gates. Every night the gates were closed and every morning they were opened. In the mornings the farmers went out in the fields and worked in their rice paddies and came back at sunset and the gates were closed. While I was there, the Chinese Nationalist Draft Board showed up, about 20 soldiers and officers. They went through the whole town and out in the fields and brought everyone from aged 15 to 30 to the center of the village, lined them up, perhaps about 100 of them, and drafted them. Every now and then someone from the village would talk to some of the officers and hand over some money, and a person was then pulled out of the line. Also, some officials from the village showed up and pulled some more people out of the line and the Chinese officers went along with it. They ended up with about 20-24 eligible men for the army. Then the soldiers produced a long rope which was roped around the necks of the chosen people, and knotted, and that was how they marched them off. At least the draft works in America a little better than that! Many people missed the Civil War by buying a substitute to go in their place. In this case, it was just a direct payment to the army officers in charge of the drafting.

There were a lot of dogs running loose in the Kunming area and the surrounding countryside. The dogs were not used to automobile traffic and GI trucks and were always getting run over. When walking, we would often make bets on how long the dead dogs would lay in the road before someone would pick him up and take him home for dinner. Dogs were a choice morsel in China, when cooked properly. A lot of Chinese people survived there on road kill.

Often, Chinese men would run in front of the trucks or the airplanes, as part of the superstition that they were being followed by a dragon or evil spirits. If they could come close enough to the front of the truck or airplane that was moving, they would get by and then the truck or plane would run over and kill the dragon. This happened hundreds of times while in a truck and I never hit one, but some people did. I witnessed one very bad accident involving a Chinese soldier. He tried to run in front of an airplane to kill the dragon behind him, but he misjudged and the propeller caught him on his right shoulder and severed him from the shoulder blade to the waist. He was still running when I saw him, and surprisingly, not bleeding much, just running like mad with his arm 90% cut off.

I saw one other bad accident on the airfield where my office was. A truck was loaded with the Chinese coolies and a P-40 landed and veered to the side and hit the truck. At least 30 people were killed and I didn't go any closer. There was nothing any of us could do.

One of the more pleasant experiences that I remember happening in China was that I did meet someone quite important to me, my cousin, Frank Brown, who was a major in the Army. He had been in the Army since he got out of the University of Illinois, about 1936, I believe. Somehow he ended up as a colonel of the MPs in Chunking. It was March of 1945 and he knew from the family where I was. We had been fairly close as children, even though he was a dozen years older than me. I looked up one day in my office and there he was. We went out and had a good time together. During one of our telephone conversations, he offered to get me transferred to Chunking with a field commission. At that time, I told him that I was already set in my ways in what I was doing. I didn't think I could do that and start over with anything else. My weight was down in the 90 pound area and the Army had begun a plan for a rotation system where you had to collect points, on how long you had been in the army, and how many months you were overseas. I had more than the needed points and in a couple of more months I would be eligible for rotation, so I thanked him told him I hoped to get rotated soon. Unfortunately, while I had the points, I never did get rotated but that's another story - later.

My Army discharge shows that I had a 72 ASR score as of September 2, 1945. The ASR was your rotation score and at that time you only had to have 60 to be rotated. It started out that you had to have 62 or something like that back in June and from then on, as more people got rotated, and the longer overseas, they cut the points down so that by the time I got 72 points and hadn't been rotated, 55 should have gotten me on my way home but things don't always work out the way you think they should. So, I stayed in Kunming.

In 1944, I met General Stilwell, our hero to many of us, while I was on the job. I had received in July a shipment of 1,000 pounds of rockets by air all the way from Miami to Kunming, to the attention of General Joseph Stilwell. They were said to be special bazooka rockets of a new armor-piercing design that would not explode when it hit but exploded later and did much more damage to the tank it hit. General Stilwell wanted to experiment with his group in Burma. The 1,000 pounds of them were in cardboard tubes and tied together. It only took about 10 days for them to arrive from Miami so I stacked them outside my office against the back wall on the platform. I tried to call Headquarters but never got through. The rockets sat there against the back wall of my office for 10 days. One day the base commander from the Air Force stormed in and wanted to know who was responsible for that ammunition piled up outside, which shouldn't have been there. He was very mad about it; he said it could have blown up the entire airfield. It was all my fault and he "chewed me out very good". He accused me and every relative I ever had of being no good and accused me of every crime possible, from being a Japanese spy to I don't know what all. He finally ended up telling me that I had at least three minutes to get those g.d. rockets off the platform and out of the way; he didn't care where I put them either. I couldn't do it in three minutes, but within an hour, I did have them loaded onto a truck and sent to the Ordinance Depot. I didn't get a court martial nor shot at dawn as the base commander had promised me. About a week later, General Stilwell showed up in my office. He asked who was in charge and asked if I had seen the rockets that were supposed to have been sent to him. I told him that the base commander had insisted I get them out of there and then he asked me where the base commander was. He said he would "take care of him" for what he had done, that the rockets should have been left here, that he still wanted them and now they were gone. He didn't blame me for anything, but he was certainly mad at the base commander. General Stilwell never did find the missing rockets, one might assume the they were shipped out to the front lines by mistake.

A week later, somebody came running in and told me General Stilwell was back and on the platform. I figured he was back looking for something new. I dashed around the corner and ran smack dab into a tall skinny man, knocked my glasses off, and I almost knocked him down. As I went by, I noticed the three stars on his collar so I tried to simultaneously do several things, none very successfully. One was to pick up my glasses and get them back on the face, salute and to apologize to General Stilwell. He straightened his glasses and his shirt, reached down and grabbed me by my upper arm and pulled me up and said "Are you all right son?" I said something to the effect of "yes sir" and tried to salute again. He was gone by then but he certainly left a great impression upon me. I wish I could thank him now but I guess I can't at this point.

In talking earlier about the Japanese almost getting into India at Kohima and Imphal, I learned this sometime after the war. There was a cemetery for British soldiers who died in the battle and the monument at the cemetery that said "we gave our today for your tomorrows." To me, that was the best memorial until the Vietnam monument was built.

I saw one large air raid which the 14th Air Force put together to bomb Japanese at Myitkyina in early 1945. The 14th collected a lot of bombers of assorted sizes, mostly B-24s and B-26s with a few pursuit planes to protect them and everybody knew they were getting ready for a big raid. It started one morning with very clear weather, taking off one at a time and once they got up in the air, they started circling until they had 24 in the air. They were flying in a large circle over Kunming. They then started to the southwest towards the Japanese lines. An hour or so later, the report came back that the raid had been completed, but it was not as successful as hoped. In fact, it was a bad mistake. The planes flew close to 24,000 feet altitude, and the lead bomber and navigator, when the time was right, led them down out of the clouds and saw a large river, which was assumed to be the Salween River. It wasn't, it was the Mekong, but Myitkyina where they were to drop the bombs was just the other side of the Salween. He led them over the Mekong River, all 24 bombers, saw a town with soldiers so they bombed the town, dropping all their bombs. The only problem was that it was a town in China, and they bombed the military installation there including the hospital. There was quite a to-do about the Chinese troops that our Air Force had killed. I don't think this was given much national publicity and I don't think that the 14th were on any other large raids staged from Kunming.

When the war came to an end after the bombs being dropped, first in Hiroshima and then on Nagasaki, our local daily news posted on the bulletin boards referred to it, but didn't say it was an atom bomb, simply said that the 10th Air Force from the Marianna Islands had dropped a super bomb on Hiroshima and blew up the whole city, including tens of thousands Japanese. The first reaction of all of us, including me, was that this was a mistake by whoever typed it. When the second one was dropped over Nagasaki, it was referred to as an atom bomb. We all realized then that the war was over, and we could forget our fears of having to go down the South China coast and getting into the shooting war that was expected there.

The Yunan Province (as mentioned previously) was ruled and controlled by a war lord, whose name was Lung Nyun. In September 1945, after the war ended, there was great fear and rumors flying around that Lung Nyun was going to use his army of one million troops which were quartered mostly around Kunming. The rumors, which had some truth to them, was that he was going to have his troops take over all our stored goods that were piled up in the depots, including the supplies that were being saved for a later invasion of China. There were millions of dollars' worth of stuff in the area, especially on the black market. To prevent this from happening, the American Air Force starting patrolling the air over Kunming and over the warlord's headquarters, which were just out of town on the edge of Lake Kunming, in a series of large white stone buildings. For the better part of a week in mid-September 1945, there were at least two P40 fighters flying circles over Kunming and over his headquarters at altitudes of 1,000 feet or less. They patrolled with two in the air 24 hours for six or seven days, until some deal was worked out about how much of the supplies would be turned over to the Nationalist Army from Chunking, General Chiang Kai-shek's army, and how much would be given to the warlord. The greater amount was going to Chiang Kai-shek, but a compromise was agreed on and the air patrol was ended.

16. <u>ROTATION</u>

The spring of 1945, the United States Army in China had started a rotation for ground troops. One was given points for the time you had been in the army, any medals you had, an extra five points for every good conduct medal, etc. The original requirement was if you had 65 points, you were available for rotation. By August of the year and after I had picked up another five points for the Bronze Star medal I was given for meritorious service, I was in the 70+ group. I was quite concerned that I had not yet shown up on the orders posted every day of the people to be rotated. So, I went to SOS Headquarters, looked around, and found the Sergeant who typed up the rotation orders. I talked to him and explained my dissatisfaction in every way I could for not being on his list. He showed me a couple of boxes on his desk of 3x5 typed cards with people's names on them. One of them was a box of cards that didn't appear to be sorted in any way (not alphabetical anyway). It was maybe 18 inches long which would have about 1,000 cards in it. He said that he was told how many people the Air Force would fly to India on the next date, and he picked that many cards out of the front of the box and typed them up and that was how people got rotated. He looked in quite a few of them for me but he didn't find me in there. He then pointed to the box alongside of it which was only about 10 inches in size and I would estimate 200-250 cards in it, which were alphabetized. He said that these were the people who were classified in their jobs as essential and that they were not be rotated. He looked under the letter "E" and I was the first one on the list, not to be rotated and was marked "essential". When he put my card back in the box, he stood it up with the short edge down. We chatted a few moments and he said he had to excuse himself to go to the 'can' and he smiled. After he left the room, I pulled my card out, which he had left sticking out on purpose, I am sure, and I put it in the box for people to be rotated. I didn't put it right in front to wave any flags; I put it maybe an inch back in the box. Sure enough, a week or so after that, the order was posted and there I was, listed for rotation for October. A lot of people then paid some attention to me. When they found out that when orders were cut at Headquarters and signed by the higher-ups, there was nothing anybody could do about it. They couldn't take it away and I started packing.

Once I was on orders to finally be rotated back to the United States after more than 600 days in Kunming, I simply got rid of everything I could, giving up clothing and anything useful to any of the people that were still working on the freight platform, and the people who had accompanied the trucks. Things that nobody wanted, I gave to the local Chinese, which they probably either wore or sold. I didn't have much else but at least I finally got rid of the sweat shirt and pants treated for gas, and weighed a ton and were never used, of course. Some poor Chinese ended up wearing them. I got rid of everything I could and then spent two or three days in a tent on the edge of the airfield where they put the people for flights to India.

In the tent next to mine, the typical four-man, eight-man tents with wooden floors and wooden rafters and tents stretched over it, was an interesting personality, a real hillbilly, who bragged about the fact that he was a backwoodsman from West Virginia. He was in the Air Force, and he had been connected to one of the Air Force photographic labs. The one thing he had and never left by itself was a rather large suitcase that would have taken probably three cubic feet to fill it. The entire contents of it were pornographic pictures and he opened it up and let people see them. I guess he would have sold some had anybody wanted to buy them. His story was that he was carefully guarding these and taking them back to West Virginia where he was going to resell them and he would then be the richest man in West Virginia when he sold these hundreds and hundreds of pornographic pictures of all kinds. One of the stacks he had was the one picture that almost every American serving in China had bought. This was a highly-doctored up picture of a complete rather fat nude Chinese girl in her early twenties. The picture had been altered so that her vagina ran crosswise (horizontal), which of course confirmed the well-known joke about Chinese women. I don't know whatever happened to my copy – I'm sure I threw it away somewhere along the line.

The other story I heard dealing with this touchy subject and it's one that I know is true because the perpetrator told me himself about it. He was a fairly young Air Force pilot who wangled a leave to India. While he was in India, he managed to get a ride to Kajahara, about 200 miles south of Calcutta, which was the area with the best known Indian temples of the sex worshippers, and there were several large temples with carved stone depicting every possible sexual act that anybody had ever thought of and most were life-sized. The Air Force man had a camera with him and he took at least 100 pictures of these sculptures. When he got back to Kunming, he carefully wrapped the pictures and mailed the package to his brother in the United States, avoiding the censors. His brother got the package around Thanksgiving. He was going to a large Thanksgiving family gathering the following Thursday, so he thought it would be a treat for everybody if he brought pictures of his little brother who was serving in the war in China and India. So, he took the package of pictures with him and when it was almost time for the family and some 20 relatives to sit down to the traditional dinner, they opened up the package. The soldier who took the pictures got some very strong letters from his mother, father and uncles. At that time, he still hadn't decided where he was going to go, but he didn't know if he dared go home again. (You got to be careful what you mail home.)

One of the big shortages in China was reading material. There was a weekly newspaper, the CBI Roundup, published in Calcutta, which had some Chinese news. From the correspondents, we kept somewhat up on the war in general. There were three available weekly magazines, and fortunately, I was one of the ones that got all three. They were overseas editions of American magazines – Time, Newsweek, and The New Yorker. These were all small, 6x9 or so, small enough to fit in an envelope. They were printed without any ads and only slightly reduced type size. Subscriptions to them sold to overseas soldier or the families of them. Usually, the magazines were delivered about two weeks after the date of the issue. I still have The New Yorker, the one which had some cartoons and a couple of stories. It was the best reading available. I always had a waiting list (among the people that worked for me) for the most recent copies of Time, Newsweek, or The New Yorker. I was the only one that I knew over there that had The New Yorker subscription.

17. COCA COLA'S FAILURE TO LIVE UP TO PROMISES MADE TO PRESIDENT ROOSEVELT OR WHY COCA COLA FAILED IN CHINA IN WWII

This is not based on today's memory but mostly on notes that I made. I started to write this up in 1970 – I felt that there was a story inside me that I had never really fully attacked or written anything about. I started writing it out and I got through seven pages of hand-written explanations, then got tired and put it in the file, and never went back to it until now.

During WWII, everyone in the United States, housewives, businesses, and everyone else had some products that were rationed. Amongst them were meat, shoes, and sugar. I think the average housewife was entitled with ration card to a half a pound of sugar a week, enough for your coffee at least. Everyone had to live up to this except the Coca Cola Company of Atlanta, which made a deal with the Government to use all the sugar they could buy without worrying about rationing. The grounds they presented successfully to the Government were that the troops in the United States and also overseas needed Coca Cola. "Coca Cola was the one thing that you needed when you came out of the foxhole, ran out of ammunition, or whatever". It was the only national soft drink in those years. The president of Coca Cola, Robert Woodruff, was a close friend of President Roosevelt, and had often stayed at the White House. He made a promise to the President of the United States, which was widely publicized in 1942, that there would be no place in the world that American soldiers could not have a <u>Coca Cola</u>. They made every effort they could to live up to this and by the end of 1944, they had gotten at least as far as into India. I was, as noted before, at the end of the Burma Road, which the Japanese had closed in 1942. At that time, there were only about 5,000 Americans total in China, of which ¾ or more were 14th Air Force. The balance was Stilwell's Y-forces and assorted other small groups.

I was then a lowly corporal that got the job of sorting and classifying all freight that the ATC brought in from India for the ground forces in C-47s, C-46s, and an occasional C-54. We had somewhere from 5 to 20 planeloads a day. I think there was one day where we had 40 and were really snowed under. I had been designated to sign for everything so that the Air Force could keep their records in order. My usual day began by my going to Air Transport Command Operations Building and to sign an original copy of the manifests, which listed everything that the planes brought in. I guess since I was a college graduate from the University of Chicago, and could obviously read and write and sign my name, the Air Freight major put me in charge of the freight operations for the ground forces. He didn't like to get up in the morning, so he wished upon me the job of signing the manifests that the goods had been received. So every morning, the first thing I did was to go to the operations shack and sign whatever manifests for planes the Air Force gave me. From letters I wrote at the time, they usually shoveled across the counter a flock of them each morning. I then had to search the cargo area for the goods listed on the illegible third copy of the manifest I was allowed to keep. Also, by then about half of the individual way bills glued to each item that had been shipped in had fallen off or were torn and the remaining ones were usually splattered or soaked in mud from the field. They weren't very readable, especially during monsoon season. That's how the supplies got to Kunming. The airplane manifest listed, by way bill, each one of the items on the plane or so they claimed, and I signed for them. I don't suppose I signed for more than a few hundred million dollars' worth of assorted goods. Once I had them in the warehouse and later on the freight platform. I had to sign a ticket for the trucks to deliver these goods to the different supply depots in the area. And so that my trucks could leave the airfield, I signed a ticket for the Chinese Army guard post at the end of the field. A ticket for the person who accompanied the truck, one of a dozen or so GIs who were working for me also had a ticket we made out. It simply said something like 65 bales of clothing for quartermaster, 200 boxes of ammunition, a lot of stuff for QM, assorted boxes for engineers, 98 pieces of truck parts for motor pool. These the person that accompanied the trucks and saw that it was delivered, had to have his ticket signed by the recipient; and brought back to me where I promptly threw them away.

My first exposure with Coca Cola in China was in the goods that Madame Chiang Kai-shek, the Dragon Lady had brought back. My count, which I had noted at that time, was 17 steamer trunks and 3 dozen open cases of Coca Cola. Her luggage and the coke were accompanied by two of the largest, meanest looking Mongolian soldiers I had ever seen. They threatened to shoot me on the spot just because after so long an absence, I wanted to caress one of the Coca Cola bottles. This was in 1944.

My next exposure to coke came in early 1945 when two large strange looking machines showed up on the loading dock. They were some kind of mixing and/or bottling machines from Coca

Cola, shipped by air all the way from Atlanta. They weighed over a ton and they were marked for the Kunming post exchange. I had them sent to the nearest PX and thought about how good a coke would taste. Also how coke would be a much better vehicle to put a little medical 190 proof grain alcohol in, which we usually just mixed with water when we got it. These two machines were soon sitting beside the PX, where they put a tarp over them. Several weeks later (it was in January when I got the coke machines); it must have been around March or early April 1945 when two mid-thirty looking executive types showed up in my office. Their khakis and tailored uniforms were strictly from Abercrombie and Fitch and their arm patches identified them as technical representatives. They carried the rank equivalent to a major and they acted like it was the equivalent of a general. They had a services of supply lieutenant and his jeep to drive them around; they had just flown in from Atlanta and were the technical reps from Coca Cola Company, and were there to set up and start the operation of a Coca Cola Bottling for the GIs in China. They said they planned to use local wine bottles for the coke because they couldn't bring the properly shaped Coca Cola bottles all the way from Atlanta. I volunteered to them that there should be quite a few empty wine bottles around because I had emptied my share of them and perhaps more in the last year plus. I gave them directions on finding the machines and off they went. I was thinking at the time that this was the end of the problem. Rather than the end, it was the beginning of two of the most hectic, threatening, and often humorous months of my life.

The next day or so, the two friendly tech reps from Atlanta were back. They thanked me for my help, said they found their machines, but there were a few parts missing. They needed some 20 or 30 feet of small sized stainless steel pipe and Monel metal stainless fittings that went with it. They wanted to know if I could direct them to it. Then the fun began.

On their second or third visit, I explained to them completely how everything worked, how we handled them, and told them that I had no idea at all anywhere about any stainless steel pipe or Monel metal fittings, etc., that if they were with the machines, they should still be with the machines. The tech reps then started on their big hunt for the Monel metal pipe. I told them, of course, to check with the quartermaster, who might have gotten them because of the markings for the PX. Also maybe they had got the engineers because they looked like engineering material pipe and we had handled a lot of pipe of other kinds or to even check the motor pool warehouses because the pipe may have looked like something that could be used on trucks. A couple of days later, they were back again, and questioned me at great length to what had I done with their stainless steel pipe and they got exactly the same explanation from me. I never saw it or didn't remember it if I did. I did not know where it was and I could suggest nothing further. They said they would look further and recheck the depots and wanted to know if there was anywhere else they could look. I told them not that I was aware of unless they wanted to check the plumbing in General Chenault's house for improvements. By then, they were beginning to become unhappy with me because I couldn't tell them where their pipe was. This was the beginning of their great life-long job to find the stainless steel pipe. On the next visit I had from the technical reps who were unhappy with my suggestions on what may have happened to the pipe and why didn't I know where it was, they made threatening suggestions that I had somehow done something with it or sold it on the black market. I explained to them that I didn't sell anything on the black market, but if I was going to, it wouldn't have been a couple of odd pieces of pipe; it would have been barrels of gasoline or bottles of pills. They came back for the fourth time, with a Lt. Colonel, who said he was my CO from the services of supply. He was not a one that I had ever seen before, but he was very pleasant and he had his aide with him. They got exactly the same story that yes, we had received the machines and I explained again that I couldn't account for their pipe and that I didn't know anything about it and that was true of any other particular article that they wanted. You could have a number of a package somewhere and I didn't have a record that told me where that package was. I said it had been delivered to where it looked like it should have gone. Next, they came back with an MP sergeant, who was a tough guy and who bought their story that I had probably black-marketed their pipe or something. He tried to convince me that if I would tell him who I sold it to, he could go get it back. Of course, he got the same story that I didn't have the slightest idea where the pipe was or what happened to it. He wasn't happy with me but there wasn't anything he could do so he left. A few days later, I got a visit from the Provost Marshal of the Kunming area and his aide. They wanted to know where the Coca Cola stainless steel pipe of these nice technical reps was. Apparently, the reps had settled in quite well in the accommodations they had been given in Hostel 1 as majors or higher. The Provost Marshal and his assistant got the same story as everybody else. I could tell them nothing more than I had told everybody else that had asked me. They kept looking and came back to see me a couple of more times in between their searches.

After the MPs did nothing for them, they contacted the CID, the criminal investigation department of the Army, who sent an officer around to talk to me. He was a pleasant guy who listened to my story, shrugged his shoulders and left. I did note at that time, though, that the tent I lived in and my foot locker, although left in good shape, had been gone through. Obviously, someone, either the CID or the technical reps thought they would go into my tent and find a bundle of money that I had gotten in the black market. Things were carefully put back in the foot locker but not quite in the way I knew they had been left. There was also an indication that some floor boards of the wooden flooring in my tent had been pried up and then nailed back down. I guess they thought I had all this money, which I didn't have or know anything about, under the floor. I also had one of the people who worked in the Army Post Office come by one day just to chat. Finally, he told me what he wanted. He wanted to know why the Coca Cola people were checking every money order that had been sent out of Kunming Post Office, the Army Post Office, in the past year. What they were looking for, of course, was all the money that wasn't under the floor of my tent or in my footlocker that I had sent home. Fortunately, from my standpoint, I hadn't sent a nickel. Bobbie got her allotment from the Government every month, which was taken out of my pay and I had never sent home any money, only a couple of minor packages that I can remember of souvenirs. They went through every one which means probably thousands of money orders, looking for the ones that I had purchased, which I had never done. So they kept coming back, getting more angry with me and they got to the point where they went to the General in charge of service supply at the time and brought his adjutant, who brought his aide down to question me. He was a most forbidding looking bird colonel but he was very pleasant and listened to the same story that I didn't have their pipe nor did I know anything about it. That was all I could say and I stuck to my story because it was the truth. They then continued on, kept making up their minds, at least in their working hours, that somehow I was out to get them and was hiding the pipe somewhere. They even got the OSS (which later became the CIA) to investigate me. One of the people who worked for me who regularly went to the one big Red Cross club in Kunming said that the Coke reps were regulars there, the two men from Atlanta in their fancy uniforms, and the ranking of major at least, made quite a hit with the twentyish years old Red Cross girls, and they were making time with them left and right. Usually the Red Cross girls never said anything but 'hello' to me because they wouldn't speak to anyone less than a field grade officer.

I don't think I had more than two days without the two tech reps bothering the heck out of me. One day, they came in with smiles on their faces, waving an airplane manifest at me, saying we have checked the manifest of every airplane that came to Kunming in the last year and here is the one with the waybill number of the package that had our pipe. So I told them again, the usual, that I never looked at a waybill, and didn't know what to do with it and I sure didn't remember anything more. They marched off and came back with the Air Corps operations officer in charge and with the manifest. He was not happy. He said he had stayed up all night with these guys while they looked through hundreds and hundreds of manifests, looking for this particular item. He simply said to me, "see, we gave it to you; it's up to you to take care of it." So I again had to repeat my story that I could not tell where that pipe was or any other item on any manifest that I had signed. Things then got funny; I got some extra help, two people who said they were just passing through. One was a very pleasant, very large, with a brogue, a former Irish cop from Boston. He said he was just killing time and was going to be sent on and that they had sent him down to learn how air freight operations were run. He wore black, high-top lace-up shoes, like a policeman would. So he followed me around with a small notebook and a pencil for about ten days, writing down everything I did. I think he even followed me to the latrine a few times, to make sure I didn't hide something back there. He was pleasant and never caused any trouble. But you do get tired of somebody breathing over your shoulder. The other one was assigned to help the guys who loaded the trucks and rode with them to see that the stuff was delivered. He didn't do more than say 'hello' to me but apparently he did question everyone who worked there about me and what did I do and what did I sell. I also had visits from officers in charge of a couple of the depots, particularly the engineering depot and the quartermaster depot. Both of them had become quite upset by their visits from the Coca Cola tech reps. They came down and asked me why I sent the tech reps to them. I said, "that's where the pipe might be". They didn't have it or know anything about it so they were in the same category as me. They weren't unpleasant about it but they weren't happy that they had to come down and listen to me trying to explain the whole thing again. Incidentally, the OSS man who had also checked me suggested "he could blow up the coke machine if I'd like him to."

This lasted altogether about six weeks. It got so that I thought it was pretty funny but the Coca Cola reps didn't agree,

I am sure. They kept telling me how important it was that one, these machines didn't go to waste and that we would all have coke and secondly, that this was necessary for their president's (Woodruff) promise to see that GIs everywhere in the world got Coca Cola. This was his solemn vow to the President of the United States, Franklin D. Roosevelt. I said that I was very sorry but I hadn't promised anything to Roosevelt except to be in the Army. It meant a great deal to them and to their careers. They disappeared for about four days and I didn't see them and I breathed a sigh of relief, after weeks of hassling. The nicer of the two of them, (they played good guy/bad guy routine on me, one would be the good guy on my side and the other played the district attorney role) the slightly older one, came in by himself one day and said that he and the other rep were leaving in a couple of days and he just wanted to see me once more and see if I couldn't give him a chance to redeem them by telling how to get the pipe and to carry out their mission. He gave me a very long story of again how important the promise to FDR was but also what it meant to him and his career. He said he certainly knew a great deal about me by then, knowing I was a college graduate. He was a college graduate also, an engineer, he was married and had two nice sons back in Atlanta in high school. If he went back to Atlanta in disgrace, he would be fired and never get another job, his family might starve, and he would never have the money to send his two sons even to the University of Georgia. He was quite emotional about all this. He actually was talking about how important it was, he somehow solved his problem and it would save his life and his family and his sons' future college education. He had tears in his eyes and I didn't see anything that could have brought this on except his emotions. I told him again that I felt sorry for him but that there was nothing I could do. I was not going to be a scapegoat or anyone, that they would just have to do whatever they wanted, but I couldn't tell them what I didn't know. I couldn't produce pipe out of thin air. After a couple of hours of listening to his sad and emotional outburst, he left and I never saw him again.

The next day, I got a visit from the other tech rep, the younger one came and told me they were leaving the next day for Atlanta and that by the following Monday, he would be in Washington, in the White House. He was giving me one last chance to cough up the truth. Again he got the same story from me, he threatened me with his connections in the White House, said that I would soon be on a plane behind them headed for Washington, where I would be court-martialed and receive at least thirty years in Leavenworth. He told me I should pack my bag and be ready to go. The only answer I could give to that was that was fine with me, it would get me out of there, I was sick of Kunming, and I would love to be in Washington next week and out of the war zone. I was just a lowly sergeant and there was nothing anybody could do to me. If I had it, I would have told him where to put it.

I had suggested to them several times that they simply order more pipe shipped by air like the original machines. They turned this down as an admission of their defeat, I guess, but they never tried to get more parts. They had more fun trying to find some way to indicate that I had taken their pipe and hidden it or sold it. It might have been easier had I done it, but I didn't.

That was the last I ever heard of the Coca Cola affair except for the next thirty years, I refused to drink a Coca Cola. I think I will send a copy of this part of my story when typed, to the Coca

Cola Company historian because I am sure they don't have my side of this horrendous story of who got the Coca Cola pipe. And I still don't know who in Kunming somewhere has some good fancy stainless steel pipe in their plumbing.

After I was awarded the Bronze Star medal for meritorious service in August 1945, the GIs who worked for me said that I got the medal for winning the battle of the war with Coca Cola. That was my prize for not giving in. Also, in connection with this, my cousin, who I mentioned earlier, was still with the MPs, with headquarters in Chunking, said that all the reports from the different people I had mentioned in the investigation of me for Coca Cola, all sent reports to the MP headquarters in Chunking, and he said they had over a file drawer full of reports on me with more coming in of the Coca Cola war and it got so that I was very well known and popular there. There was betting what the final outcome would be and how many reports would come in the next day about me, etc. He said they had over a full file cabinet drawer of these reports and he told people I was his cousin. He was kidding about what his cousin did with the pipe so I was pretty well known in military police headquarters theater at the time, although I would prefer not to believe that was the only reason I got my bronze star medal.

18. <u>OTHER WAR MEMORIES</u>

In the late summer of 1944, after I had my meetings and run into General Stilwell, both business-wise, with his rockets and physically hitting him coming around the corner, some of the people picked up the idea that I should be called Vinegar Joe, I was not as tall as he but I was skinnier. I obviously admired the man so they started calling me "Vinegar Joe" as a nickname which stuck with me to the end. When people would kid me about it, they would say, okay now Vinegar Joe Evans, or Sergeant Vinegar Joe. There just has to be some humor somewhere during wartime.

In late 1944, I was given the task of putting together several loads at different times, mostly ammunition, medical supplies, small arms, and occasionally clothing and food, to be dropped to Ho Chi Minh's forces, in what was then French Indo-China near Hanoi. They were being supported and had some training by the OSS, the Office of Strategic Services, which was a hush hush spy type organization. It was the organization that later became, and still is, the CIA, Criminal Investigation. So, I saw the beginning of the CIA, as OSS. People did mention him and whether he was in China or not, I don't know, but the OSS was headed by "Wild Bill Donovan", who built this organization. The ones I knew were all quite healthy and active tough guys. They were the ones that flew over Hanoi and into that area. Some of them parachuted into the area and others just flew in and pushed the goods out of the airplane that were shipped to the forces. The reason for part of this was that Ho Chi Minh was well known as a disciple or someone who was extremely fond of Abraham Lincoln, his idol. The important thing was that he had the only army that was actively regularly fighting the Japanese in Asia at that time. Chinese troops, as I mentioned before hadn't fought much since 1939, almost until we entered the war. Ho Chi Minh had his army fighting the Japanese, and this was essentially the beginning of the army that drove the French out of Indo-China and when it was called Viet Nam, they were responsible for getting the Americans out in a war that we really lost. The drops to Hanoi were all done by the 322nd troop carrier squadron, which at this time, in 1944, was stationed in Kunming. Their airplanes consisted of several, maybe as many as half a dozen C-47s (DC-3s), except that they had a large double door a little over halfway back between the wings and the tail. These double doors had been removed so that they could push out wooden platforms with goods strapped to them, even 75 millimeter guns, etc. How well they flew with big openings in them, I don't know, but they never had the doors on them closed that I could see. Several times, I was given by OSS people lists of goods to make up or that were already marked for them when we received them on the freight platform.

One incident I remember too well because it scared the life out of me was that I told my crew putting the loads together for me to fix up a couple of loads for Hanoi – we simply labeled them for the OSS. I looked out later and they had these goods set aside, which consisted mostly of ammunition and some medical supplies and some small arms. They had the two trucks sitting there loaded. A few hours later and noticed that the two trucks, each with a load of approximately 3,000 pounds or a little more were gone. I asked the people what had happened to them. They told me that the 322nd people came and picked them up and one of my men went with them to where they loaded them on an airplane. They said they loaded both trucks onto a DC-3 of the 322nd. Then I almost fainted; when I had told them to make up the two loads, I had assumed they would realize these were two loads for two airplanes; instead a single DC-3 was loaded with a double load, well over 6,000 pounds. The plane must have had a great pilot and it managed to get off the ground. I checked on it as soon as I could with Airport Control. The plane completed its mission and safely returned. How an old DC-3 could take off at over 6,000 feet with double the load that they were supposed to be able to carry, I will not ever understand, but I was very glad that the wonderful airplane was able to do it and that it just didn't break down and crash on the runway due to twice the amount of weight in it that it should have had. The GIs that were working for me on the platform heard about it in a lot of ways and were told to watch in the future and never do anything that I didn't approve of. At least the outcome was good.

Another thing about the 322nd that surprised me (and some of them must have been pretty hot pilots) at least twice when they came back, one or two of their DC-3 planes made for dropping goods, did aerobatics with the DC-3s like the British fighter pilots had done. They would zoom in on the field and up into a half-loop and maybe a barrel roll as they came out of the loop, and then go around and land. They did this early in the time they were there. I imagine somebody gave them orders not to after that, but it was quite a sight to see a DC-3 going into a loop. It reminded me of an air show I had seen when I was in high school in Florida, where the height and the biggest part of the air show was an old Ford Tri-motor doing a loop. Considering the weight on them and other things, this was an even greater air show. I hope those pilots are still flying – I would like to fly with them some day.

In November or December of 1944, while I was temporarily living in Hostel 7 on the eastern edge of Kunming, one Sunday I watched a defeated Chinese army coming down the road. The first of them were visible when we got up that morning around 7:00. These were all foot soldiers, all walking, no trucks or transportation and almost all of them had injuries. Many of them were two soldiers sort of carrying between them a third who was on one foot. Many of them had crutches and more were using their rifles like a crutch. They were all Nationalist Army and they were all in uniforms as they came down this gravel road past Hostel 7. They were maybe four or five across and were going at a slow walking pace because most of them had visible injuries, ranging from burns and bandages on their bodies and a great many of them had open sores on their legs. One of our interpreters went out and talked to some of them as they went by, and he said that the reason so many of them had burns was that before the Japanese had routed this army, they had gone over the fields behind them and sprayed those fields with mustard gas the night before. Then they attacked the army which was dug in, facing the Japanese, and routed them. When they retreated, they went through these fields, bushes, rice paddies that still had mustard gas, which caused all these burns. This procession of Chinese soldiers was about a pitiful sight as you could ever imagine. It went on from dawn to dusk that day. You couldn't count them, but there must have been at least 20,000 or more of them, defeated and dragging themselves back to Kunming. Hopefully, some of them got to hospitals and were treated. It was not a pleasant sight to see, and difficult to remember now many years later.

By September (as noted earlier), in 1945, I was doing everything to get myself out of China and home. I had plenty of points to do it, although I had been classified as essential. I was at that time offered a last chance for promotion to first lieutenant if I would sign up for another six months in China, with promises of going to Shanghai or some such place to set up an air freight operation, which naturally I turned down because I simply wanted to go home. I then wangled myself out of the essential group into a list of those being sent back to the United States. I did get my orders to go back to the United States in late October of 1945.

The last thing I did besides saying goodbye to my crew was that on my way to the camp where there were tents of people waiting for the flight to India, I drove the jeep I had been using for the past few months up to the PX, where the coke machine was still sitting, and the tarp covering it was torn and parts of the machines was rusted. I got out of the jeep, faced the Coca Cola machine and saluted it, got back in the jeep, went to the camp for the plane to India, turning the jeep over to one of the people I had left behind who was still working the air freight.

19. GOING HOME!

I spent a couple of days waiting for the plane to India and managed to get myself on a C-54 for a direct flight to the Calcutta area, to the airport at Barrackpore about 30 miles outside Calcutta. I was there for about eight or nine days and I can recall only a couple of things from that time. One was two trips in a hired taxi with three other sergeants splitting the costs. We went to Calcutta to eat and drink and had a pretty good time. We rode around in rickshaws and other things that tourists did. Our tents there were open-sided because of the extreme heat. Daily temperatures went up to the upper 100's or more. As the sides of the tents were rolled up, whatever breezes there were went right through the tent. In the tent where I was, there was a little baby monkey, maybe a month old, and I fed him. I would bring him some rice or bread, or meat, and put it on my bed. He would appear from somewhere and eat. He would never let me pick him up but he seemed to always be waiting for me to bring him his lunch or dinner. Several nights when it was cold, I would wake up in the night and find that he had crawled under the blanket with me to stay warm. I continued to feed it until I left. I assume he adopted somebody else after I was gone but it was really an odd kind of occurrence.

Also, this was the first time I had ever seen any air spraying of DDT, which was very common in India in 1945 and common in the United States until outlawed. At least twice a day, DC-3s, equipped with spraying equipment, flew over this camp and the airport, spraying DDT, heavy enough so that when you saw them coming, you ran inside because if you stayed out in it, you would choke on it. It kept the place mosquito-free and they were obviously worried about malaria because even though we were all leaving, we got the usual treatment in the mess line; you couldn't go ahead to get your food until you swallowed your atabrine tablet. So I spent a little better than a week there and finally on November 8, we were taken down river on an Army transportation landing craft, a whole group of us, to the port part of Calcutta and were loaded on a troop ship, designated as an AP, armed personnel or something like that. It was about 375 to 380 feet long and looked a little bit like a destroyer, except it was made simply to carry troops. Inside the holds of the ship were nothing but four-tiered bunks about 16 inches apart, with aisles so narrow you had to pretty well go through them sideways. We were told there were close to 2,000 troops crammed into it. We were fed twice a day in the mess halls on the ship, standing up, because they didn't want to waste the time of having to use space for somebody to sit, so we stood up to eat and it didn't take long. The food was edible, but nothing to brag about and twice a day seemed to keep everybody alive. We sailed from Calcutta the next morning down the Bay of Bengal. After a couple of days, we pulled into the harbor at Colombo Ceylon (now Sri Lanka), and took on fuel. With 2,000 GIs on the ship, they decided not to let any of us off, as if someone would desert to Ceylon while they were on their way home. I did get a good view of the port and the mountain in the background. Ceylon was the CBI theater headquarters and had a lot of publicity during the war.

After a day or so, we sailed off into the Indian Ocean where I remember just one thing that was different. We sailed for at least 36 hours through a sea of jellyfish, most of them about the size of my hand, maybe 8 inches across, but billions of them. You couldn't see the ocean for the jellyfish. The bow wave looked like it was cutting through solid jellyfish for an area of at least 300 miles. After a day or two, maybe three, we entered the Red Sea from the Indian Ocean, and proceeded up to the end of the Suez Canal to the town of Suez. It was a large port full of boats of all kinds, military to Arab dhows, little fishing boats, where they were still getting pearls out of the Red Sea. We proceeded through the Suez Canal and to the town of Port Said at the Mediterranean end of the Canal.

One thing I noted at the time was that near Port Said, where the Canal widened out, there were maybe 8 or more old freighters that looked like they were permanently anchored, not on the shore but close to it, and they were loaded with refugees. These were all Jewish refugees from southern Europe and from the death camps. At that time, the British were not letting them go into what later became Israel. They were crammed on these ships, from babies to very elderly, and had laundry draped over the side. They all waved at us but they didn't seem to be happy. I imagine a good many of them managed to swim to land; they weren't more than 100 yards out. We were told that some of them had been held there already for six months or more from when they were let loose from their German prison camps. These boat loads really started the country that is now Israel.

We steamed on through the Mediterranean, saw some of the shoreline of Africa, saw Sicily as we went by, maybe five miles away, and sailed on to Gibraltar, which looked just like the pictures, a big rock with a lot of fortifications on it and out into the Atlantic, headed towards New York. About the time or shortly after we entered the Atlantic, we ran into part of a storm that was one of the worst that they had ever seen in the North Atlantic. Some might remember pictures of one of our aircraft carriers that had the whole landing front deck of it turned up 90 degrees from the waves of this November storm of the AP I was on. At least 90% of the passengers, (the GIs) were seasick and these strong winds which were averaging 60 to 70 mph, had the AP listing to port, about 18 degrees. It was difficult to walk on the deck – you could get around if you hung onto something between each step but it was like living on a side of a hill. You got a lot more food at the time because none of the seasick people would go to their meals. The navy cooks were glad to see somebody at the evening meal. You would show up and find only a few people in the mess hall. Fortunately, from my boating experience, I didn't get seasick. The name of the AP was Adolph Greely, an Arctic explorer.

20. **BACK IN THE U.S.A.**

On December 6, 1945 (the dates on my discharge), we sailed into New York Harbor, and were met on the docks by all kinds of Red Cross people, most of them with big carts full of little half-pint cartons of milk, the reason being everybody thought that was what Americans were starved for. I didn't want any white milk and I couldn't find anybody with beer so I simply got on the train that took us all to Fort Dix, New Jersey to await transportation to a separation center.

I left from California and came back in New York. The one souvenir I have from the trip was towards the end of it, we were given certificates that stated we had gone around the world, sort of like crossing the Equator certificate that I had years before. We took a train from the dock at New York's side of the Hudson, to Fort Dix, New Jersey. As best I can remember was maybe an hour or an hour and a half train trip. I was assigned to a barrack and everybody got a steak dinner for new arrivals. The surprising thing to me was that all the people serving the food, cooking the food, and cleaning up around Fort Dix were all German army prisoners. Confronting yourself with the enemy, even though they were prisoners, was difficult for many people to take, although you finally realized these were just young people like ourselves who happened to be on the other side. They seemed to enjoy what they doing; they looked well-fed and happy. After eating, I immediately headed to a PX where there was beer and managed to drink several bottles of beer, which turned out to be Old Style Lager, one I was very familiar with, as my father had been one of the people that ran Old Style in Wisconsin, as well as Burghoff Beer in Indiana. He was a vice president and director of Old Style, and there I was greeted with it, getting a large supply of it at 10 cents a bottle, and very cold. It suited me just fine.

One other occurrence at Fort Dix that I remember was the only time I used my rank to get something done. After I had been promoted to sergeant back in the spring, and because of my previous experience when I was only a corporal, I decided I was not going to "pull rank." The usual way was in dealing with anybody with less rank was to point to the number of stripes on your arm and I had never done that with people working for me. I had an occasion in Fort Dix where I did do this and I was glad that I did. The next day, I went to get a GI haircut with GI barbers giving people their fast seven minute crewcuts with electric clippers. In the chair next to me was a very young soldier, who had apparently come in the ETO recently, getting his hair cut. He looked like he was about 15 or 16 years old, although he should have been 18 to have been in the army. The barber was just about through cutting his hair, and was hassling the kid something terrible to let him shampoo his head for 30 cents. He kept verbally brow-beating the young man and the young GI kept telling the barber that he only had 25 cents and he needed that for a telephone call to his home. This just made the barber try harder to get the last quarter out of this young soldier so he could put it in his pocket. I listened to him haranguing and threatening and telling this young man all the possible terrible things that would happen if he didn't get the foreign lice from his scalp. I had enough. I leaned over and looked at the barber and said, "Quit picking on that kid," in as loud and mean a voice as I could and added, "and don't say another word to him; just cut his hair." I then pointed to the stripes on my arm. The barber muttered "yes sarge" a couple of times but went ahead and didn't say a word more, just finished cutting the young soldier's hair. When I got out of the barber shop about four minutes later, the young man was waiting for me out front. He thanked me profusely a couple of times for getting the barber off his neck and all I could tell him was to forget it and good luck and to make his phone call.

I then started waiting for the train that was going to take me to Camp Grant, a large army camp in Rockford, Illinois, which was the separation center for the Midwest. It was a two-day train ride, regular Pullman cars. Fortunately, I got an upper berth so I didn't have to share with anybody, spent two days with all the tests and paperwork and even some pay to be discharged. My discharge shows that I was given what was due me the past month and I got a cash payment of $269.28 for my final pay from the army.

After we got through with all the paperwork, they had sort of a graduation ceremony where everybody walked by and got their discharge with their name on it. I noticed a big rubber stamp on the back of the envelope you were given to put your discharge in, which I still have, were the words to *God Bless America*, and everybody had to stand up in the auditorium when we got the discharge and sing and then we were free men. I took what I had left, half a barrack's bag of junk, clothing, and headed for Chicago on a train. I had a free ticket to Chicago, and went to the South Shore Country Club in Chicago, where Bobbie was waiting for me. She already had a room set aside for us and she brought along the suitcase of clothes that I had sent her when I was inducted in the Army back in April of 1943 at Fort Custer, Michigan in a suitcase and she had saved them and brought them along. I went upstairs to our room, took off my uniform, put on my civvies and never put on a uniform of any kind since then. I was then officially and finally what we always answered when somebody said "what do you want to be after you're in the army, what do you want to be after the war", and the standard answer, mine included of course, was "Civilian", and that I was.

21. FINAL 'ARMY' THOUGHTS

This is the end of my autobiography of WWII, as I saw it. The question has been raised and I mentioned one instance where it was suggested that the whole China thing was not valuable. However, from what I have read and studied, and my small part in it, the good thing about being in China, the famous airlift over the Hump, was that without this much danger from the Americans and our intervention, we kept the Japanese from removing their troops from the China mainland. The Japanese had one to two million troops in China all the way from Manchuria down to French Indo-China. If we hadn't been in China, those Japanese troops would have been fighting Americans in the South Pacific. Whether the cost of 500, 600 – less than 1,000 airplanes, bringing things over the Hump, and unfortunately, 3,000 or so American deaths was worth that or not, I cannot say. It was, to me, in some ways, an interesting experience, as all my army days were. The main memories of it were loneliness and boredom, but I tried to carry my share of the load and putting all this on tape has been a difficult job reliving and has made me think a lot about these things that I had pretty well put in the background for the last almost 57 years. I learned a lot; I lived in a feudal society; I learned about other people; I had some interesting experiences; I certainly had a changed personality in some ways from when I left, as a happy-go-lucky playboy from a rich family, I came home a lot different person and fortunately, I had a wonderful woman, my wife Bobbie, waiting for me and we were together for the next almost 56 years.

The one souvenir I still have is my Army blouse, like a suitcoat, although it's size 34 and I will never get in that again.

On the left side, over the pocket are five bars which are related to medals I collected. The first one was a Bronze Star medal for meritorious service; the other award type is simply the Good Conduct Medal, which about probably at least one percent of all GIs got somewhere or other; the third is the Asiatic-Pacific theater bar and medal with two battle-stars for the two times we were considered in battle area; and the fourth medal is the American Campaign Medal, which I mentioned earlier from serving with the Navy on the Liberty Ship armed guard. The last medal is the WWII Victory Medal. (These are bars for all five of the medals in a frame that I still have.) On the left arm of the coat, starting at the top, is a CBI patch, a sun and star in white on a blue top and red and white stripes. Under the CBI patch; and on both arms are the three stripes with a 4 under them for my rank; and at the bottom, near the end of the sleeve, are four gold colored bars with red thread, each approximately an inch and a half long, which are for overseas service, two years I spent overseas. Below that is about a 2 ¼ to a 2 ½ inch bar on an angle, a khaki colored bar with a black border around it for having served more than three years in the Army, which was known in the Army as an "old fogey". On the right side of the uniform, above the pocket is the one thing I had looked for a long time, the thing that indicates you were discharged, it was sewed on the uniform and also we had a pin. It was called a "ruptured duck" and it meant that you were no longer in service and honorably discharged. On the collar there is the insignia on the left, cross-cannons for the field artillery and the one on the right in large letters, U.S. Inside, in heavy India ink, are my last four numbers which is how we marked our laundry, E1054, the last of my serial numbers.

This is the last of my recording, which amount to about ten hours. I won't say it's been fun recording them because it has brought back too many memories that had been pretty well buried, but I am not sorry I was in the Army. I did what I could and my future generations can judge whether this is worth reading or not. I won't be around to know so it won't matter. I have tried to give a good picture of an individual's views of the war and what I saw and hopefully some that I had learned and that certainly affected me the rest of my life.

I served the United States Army 968 days, 737 of these were overseas.

22. EPILOGUE

In 1998 and 1999, Tom Brokaw, a famous NBC correspondent, published two of books entitled <u>Greatest Generations</u> where he implies that the generation that was in the war in 1939 to 1945 represented the greatest generation in our history. I find this quite flattering but I can't really agree with him that my generation was the greatest the Country ever saw. There are two kinds of greatness, in a sense. One, in terms of people, there are people who are born to be great leaders and would be, no matter what generation or time they were born in. In my days, on the side of what I would call good leaders were certainly our President, Franklin D. Rooselvelt, Winston Churchill in England, probably Charles De Gaulle in France. On the side of the bad, but still people who would have been leaders regardless were Adolph Hitler, Joseph Stalin, and the tyrant Chinese dictator, Chiang Kai-shek. I don't think the Japanese Emperor alone should rate that high but some of the Japanese militarists might. The rest of us were simply products of our situation and we happened to be there. We didn't choose it and it didn't choose us. Had we not had the war, nobody would have called us the greatest.

The one thing that is seldom mentioned these days is that those of us who served in WWII always knew that we were backed by the Country. As I think back on it now, I cannot remember ever hearing a single person in the military suggest that we could lose the war. We were confident we would win the war and that America would produce everything necessary so that it was won. The people in the homeland really didn't complain about gasoline or sugar ration cards. This was a time when the women in the United States came to the front, took over the men's jobs in the factories when the men went to war. We are not the greatest generation except for the true leaders. We are the products of time, the fact that we were there. We didn't fight any harder because we were born during the depression or something like that. We just happened to be there and we didn't have any choice except to do what we did. I still appreciate and enjoy war books, but I really don't think we deserve the adulation of any kind. We were just doing what the situation told us to.

To my future generations that happen to run across some copies of this, I hope that you will think some part of it is "ding hao." To my direct descendants, you are free if you want to, and if you enjoy some of this, may think of me as simply "Sergeant Vinegar Joe Evans'. I might prefer that you thought of me as retired Professor Emeritus from Northwestern University, who also taught at University of Chicago and University of Hawaii, but the fact that someone may have some memory is rewarding to me. To my descendants who certainly have my eternal love, all I can say is "it's time for me to go have a shot of Jing Bao juice." I will hoist the glass up and say "Gham-Bei" (cheers).

September 28, 2002
Nashville, Tennessee
(Transcription completed July 6, 2003)

God Bless and Good Night.

23. SOURCE MATERIAL

For the past fifty-seven (57) years, I have purchased and read every book I could find that dealt with our part of the war in China. None of them treated it as I have in any way, and most of them dealt with politics or the big picture or battles. I have ten books only, which I guess proves the most common saying about the forces in CBI and particularly in China, was that "Nobody knows we're here and Nobody cares we're here." Of the list of the books that I have, the best one was really the first one written, in 1946, it is <u>Thunder Out of China</u>, by Theodore White and Anna Lee Jacobi. It is the best story of what happened and written quite soon after it happened. The second one that I have is <u>The Stilwell Papers,</u> which Stilwell himself put together but they were arranged and edited by Theodore White and this was published in 1948. It was quite factual but very political. A third volume I have is called simply <u>The Hump</u>, by Bliss K. Thorn, which was published in 1965, which is a book with some pretty good pictures of mostly the Hump, what it was like to fly it and all of the things that went with it. The fourth book in my collection is Barbara Tuchman's book, <u>Stilwell and The American Experience in China, 1911 to 1945</u>, and was published in 1970. Tuchman was a very well-known author who had written several books – historical books. Her best-known book I suppose, published in the 60's was <u>The Guns of August</u>. Her Stilwell book has some parts that have oft been quoted (and with which I disagree), find that on page 499, she says that,

"The option to end support to China was almost taken. More from the general dissatisfaction than far-seeing policy, the joint chiefs considered the alternative of abandoning the line over the Hump and as Stimpson recorded giving up for the present 'aiding China at all.' They were forced to conclude, however that this would have such a bad effect on China's morale. The decision was bitter because the feeling that the long run effort over the Hump, the supplies to Chenault had been wasted and as Stimpson wrote, it was likely to cost an extra winter in the main theater of the war."

Also, later in the paragraph,

"although Chenault had been given almost twice as much in the way of equipment over the Hump as he asked for, he was unable to stop any Japanese while Stilwell has proved the only success on the whole horizon and the CBI was being made a victim."

The fifth book I have is called The Eagle Against the Sun, by Ronald H. Specter, and was published in 1985, about the American war with Japan that has some references to the war in China, but not a lot. The next book in my collection was published in 1992 and is called Burma Victory. It deals mostly with the situation in Burma and really ends with the final British victory in Imphal and Kohima, that I almost fought in but talked about earlier. The seventh book in my collection is called Flying the Hump, Memories of an Air War, by Otha Spencer about one person's view of flying the Hump in China and oriented completely towards the Air Force, but interesting and a pretty good amount of information of the war. Then there are items eight and nine of my list, two volumes of the Oxford Press. First is the Oxford Companion to WWII, which was published in 1995 and it has approximately 1,350 pages, of which maybe a dozen or so deal with China. An other book of my collection is the Oxford Companion to American Military History, edited by John Chambers, II, and it was published in 1999. The tenth book on my shelf is Born to fly the Hump by Dr. Carl Frey Constein (First Books, 2001). Great flying of the Hump, 96 round trips, But he never once got into Kunming city.

So my war was not as large as I had thought, but this was true of the whole CBI. The estimates were maybe 50,000-60,000 Americans total in the China Burma-India theater during WWII. My version of the CBI is number 11, after these ten that I have saved.

In addition to these ten volumes I have just listed, I have two small paperbacks that were published by the War and Navy Departments of the United States, Washington, D.C. One is a Pocket guide to India; the second is a Pocket guide to China. Both are about 70 pages, 4 x 5 size, and full of a lot of mistakes, like telling us the only language needed in China was Mandarin, and listing a vocabulary in it, which was an official language but not used by anybody except maybe in Chunking.

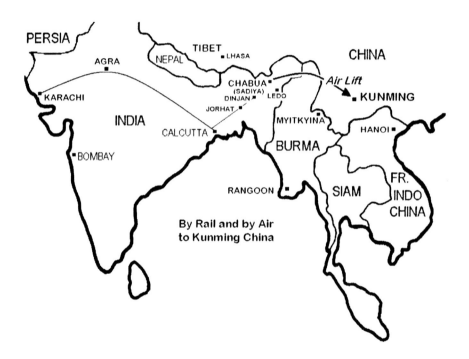

By Rail and by Air to Kunming China

24. PHOTOS

India	-	**11**
China	-	**41**
Personal	-	**13**
Misc.	-	**14**

Barber 'shop'

Death in the street

Sikh Taxi

Fakir - (Holy Man)

```
FIRPO'S SERVICES RESTAURANT

        Meatless Day

                                     As.
Egg Sandwich                          3
Tomato Sandwich                       2
2 Fried Eggs & Chip Potatoes          8
Fish & Chip Potatoes                 12
Fish Cakes & Chip Potatoes           10
Plain Omelette                        8
Omelette and Chip Potatoes           10
Macaroni Tomato sauce                 6
Fried Eggs, Each                      2
Bread & Butter   (2 Slices)           1
Mince Pies                            4
Puddings (different
               kinds daily)           4
Pot of Tea   (per person)             3
Coffee with Sugar and Milk
               (per cup)              2
Fresh Lemon Squash                    2
Beer per qrt.          Rs. 1-2-0


Note:Menu From Firpo's
     Best English Restaurant in
     Calcutta, on Chowringee Blv.
     As = Annas   about 3 cents

        India 1944
```

Note:Menu From Firpo's Best English Restaurant in Calcutta, on Chowringee Blv. As = Annas about 3 cents India 1944

Calcutta

Calcutta Harbor

Ging Po Gate

Kunming China 1944 - 45

Kunming

Kunming 1944

Traffic Cop

Kunming China '44

Kunming China

Temple

Yo-Yo Pole & Baskets   -   Kunming

C.N. (Chinese National) official rate 200 = 1 US dollar

By war's end inflated to 3000 = 1

C.N. (Chinese National)
C.N. (Chinese National) official rate 200 = 1 US dollar
By wars end inflated to 3000 = 1

Tail Fin (Japanese Bomb) Picked up 100 yds. from my office

By Cart and By Boat

Leper, Kunming 1944

Kunming 1944

News of the day

C-46 Kunming Air Port Alt. 6240'

Kunming '44

Ging Po Gate

New cigarettes from used butts, nothing was wasted

Kunming River

Meat Market

Pony Carts

Bombed Village at end of Airport Runway

Farmers   Kunming, China   1944

Camel-back Bridge   Ta-Kuan Park

Downtown Kunming 1944 - 45

Draw Bridge - Kunming River

Death takes no holiday in China

Stand in the park

Kunming China

Minnow Netting

Sail Power, Kunming '45

Kunming, Yunnan Province, China 1944

Kunming Street '44 - '45

Jing Po Gate - Kunming '44

Suez canal

Port Said - Suez Canal 1945

Barbara Both & Franklin B. Evans Sept. 16, 1943 The first of 54 years

Tech 4 Franklin B. Evans

F.B. Evans in China

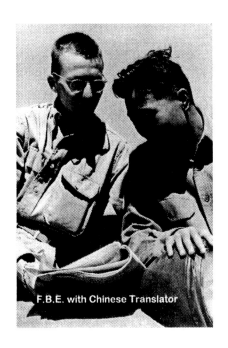

F.B.E. with Chinese Translator

F.B.E. Dec. 1944 wt. 102 lbs.

F. B. Evans in China 1944 - 1945 (above and below)

F. B. Evans in China 1944 - 1945

"Vinegar Joe" Evans

Free postcard to tell your family you are headed over seas.

Savings War Bond of India.

Purchased at Post Office on 2-21-1944 Calcutta, India

Cost 10 Rupees – ($3.50) After 12 years worth 15 Rupees

Government of India would still, probably make good

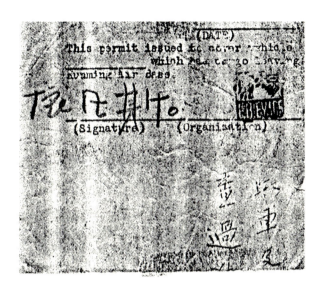

Gate Pass For truck to get off Air Field.
My signature on 'Chop' needed. I signed at least 5,000 plus.

Honorable Discharge

This is to certify that

FRANKLIN B EVANS

Army of the United States

is hereby Honorably Discharged from the military service of the United States of America.

This certificate is awarded as testimonial of Honest and Faithful Service to this country.

Given at   SEPARATION CENTER
               CAMP GRANT   ILLINOIS

Date   12 DECEMBER 1945   *Paul J Ritchie*
                                               PAUL J RITCHIE
                                               LT COL INF

ENLISTED RECORD AND ... — HONORABLE DISCHARGE

BOOK 131 PAGE 98

1. LAST NAME—FIRST NAME—MIDDLE INITIAL	2. ARMY SERIAL NO.	3. GRADE	4. ARM OR SERVICE	5. COMPONENT
EVANS FRANKLIN B	16 081 054	TEC 4	FA	AUS

6. ORGANIZATION	7. DATE OF SEPARATION	8. PLACE OF SEPARATION
HQ & HQ CO. SOS	12 DEC 45	SEPARATION CENTER CAMP GRANT ILL

9. PERMANENT ADDRESS FOR MAILING PURPOSES	10. DATE OF BIRTH	11. PLACE OF BIRTH
6714 BENNETT AVE CHICAGO ILL	9 FEB 1922	CHICAGO ILL

12. ADDRESS FROM WHICH EMPLOYMENT WILL BE SOUGHT	13. COLOR EYES	14. COLOR HAIR	15. HEIGHT	16. WEIGHT	17. NO. DEPEND
SEE 9	BROWN	BROWN	5-7½	128	1

18. RACE	19. MARITAL STATUS	20. U.S. CITIZEN	21. CIVILIAN OCCUPATION AND NO.
WHITE / NEGRO X / OTHER	SINGLE X / MARRIED / OTHER	YES X / NO	STUDENT BUSINESS ADMINISTRATION X-02

MILITARY HISTORY

22. DATE OF INDUCTION	23. DATE OF ENLISTMENT	24. DATE OF ENTRY INTO ACTIVE SERVICE	25. PLACE OF ENTRY INTO SERVICE
18 AUG 42		29 APR 43	CHICAGO ILL

26. SELECTIVE SERVICE DATA	27. LOCAL S.S. BOARD NO.	28. COUNTY AND STATE	29. HOME ADDRESS AT TIME OF ENTRY INTO SERVICE
REGISTERED YES / NO X		COOK ILL	5639 UNIVERSITY AVE CHICAGO ILL

30. MILITARY OCCUPATIONAL SPECIALTY AND NO.	31. MILITARY QUALIFICATION AND DATE
CLERK GENERAL 055	MM WITH M1 RIFLE

32. BATTLES AND CAMPAIGNS
CHINA INDIA BURMA

33. DECORATIONS AND CITATIONS
1 SERVICE STRIPE 4 OVERSEAS SERVICE BARS AMERICAN CAMPAIGN MEDAL ASIATIC PACIFIC THEATER RIBBON W/2 BRONZE BATTLE STARS GOOD CONDUCT MEDAL BRONZE STAR (106 SOS USF) WORLD WAR II VICTORY MEDAL

34. WOUNDS RECEIVED IN ACTION
NONE

35. LATEST IMMUNIZATION DATES				36. SERVICE OUTSIDE CONTINENTAL U.S. AND RETURN		
SMALLPOX	TYPHOID	TETANUS	OTHER	DATE OF DEPARTURE	DESTINATION	DATE OF ARRIVAL
IM NOV 45	STIM JAN 45	STIM JUL 43		25 NOV 43	CBI	18 JAN 44
				8 NOV 45	USA	6 DEC 45

37. TOTAL LENGTH OF SERVICE				38. HIGHEST GRADE HELD
CONTINENTAL SERVICE		FOREIGN SERVICE		
YEARS	MONTHS DAYS	YEARS	MONTHS DAYS	
1	3 13	2	0 12	TEC 4

39. PRIOR SERVICE
NONE

40. REASON AND AUTHORITY FOR SEPARATION
CONV OF GOVT RR 1-1 (DEMOBILIZATION) AR 615-365 DATED 15 DEC 44

41. SERVICE SCHOOLS ATTENDED	42. EDUCATION (Years)
NONE	GRAMMAR 8 / HIGH SCHOOL 4 / COLLEGE 4

PAY DATA VOU 174523

43. LONGEVITY FOR PAY PURPOSES			44. MUSTERING OUT PAY		45. SOLDIER DEPOSITS	46. TRAVEL PAY	47. TOTAL AMOUNT, NAME OF DISBURSING OFFICER
YEARS	MONTHS	DAYS	TOTAL	THIS PAYMENT			
3	3	25	300	100	NONE	4.40	269.28 G F DOLBEAR CAPT FD

INSURANCE NOTICE

48. KIND OF INSURANCE	49. HOW PAID	50. Effective Date of Allotment Discontinuance	51. Date of Next Premium Due (One month after 50)	52. PREMIUM DUE EACH MONTH	53. INTENTION OF VETERAN TO
Nat. Serv. X / U.S. Govt.	Allotment X / Direct to VA	31 DEC 45	31 JAN 46	6.50	Continue X / Cease

54. REMARKS
LAPEL BUTTON ISSUED
ASR SCORE (2 SEP 45) 72 Rotation Points
INACTIVE STATUS ERC 18 AUG 42 TO 28 APR 43

55. SIGNATURE OF PERSON BEING SEPARATED
Franklin B. Evans

56. PERSONNEL OFFICER (Type name, grade and organization – signature)
ELLA L WRIGHT 1ST LT WAC

FRANKLIN B EVANS

To you who answered the call of your country and served in its Armed Forces to bring about the total defeat of the enemy, I extend the heartfelt thanks of a grateful Nation. As one of the Nation's finest, you undertook the most severe task one can be called upon to perform. Because you demonstrated the fortitude, resourcefulness and calm judgment necessary to carry out that task, we now look to you for leadership and example in further exalting our country in peace.

Harry Truman

THE WHITE HOUSE

Original V-Mail from, China 1944

C. N. Chinese Nat. currency

Jacket Patches

F.B.E. Medals

1 Lake Grove,
Coburg N13
Vic. Australia
17th Dec. 1956

Dear Frank,
  Well, another year has passed nearly 11 years since I last saw you in Kunming, China. A lot of water has passed under the bridge since that time but I ~~can never forget your kindness~~ to me, A Chinese in his own country, yet more of stranger than you were.
  I am no letter writer and this is my once a year effort, but always bear in mind that I will always remember you.
  Xmas greetings to you and your family.
            Sincerely Yours
               George Lau

Hawaii Tribune-Herald, Wednesday, October 9 2002
Hawaii report

Honolulu- An Army search team has returned to Hawaii with what are believed to be remains of four U.S. service members killed in a World War II-era plane crash about 15,500 feet up the Himalayan Mountains, officials said.

The team from the Army's Central Identification Laboratory, Hawaii, also gathered information from a second WWII-era crash site higher up the mountains to help lab researchers connect the site to three other missing American service members, the Army said Monday.

The 14-member team left for Tibet in August on a mission searching for remains of four people who were aboard a C-46 transport plane that was reported missing in flight from Kunming, China, to its home base at Sookerating, India, in March 1944. It was believed to have run out of fuel before crashing into a ravine about halfway up the mountain.

Near the end of that mission, a four-member team broke off from the main team to search the second site at about 16,200 feet. The second crash also involved a C-46 aircraft, although it is unknown exactly how many people were aboard that flight

(Note: Hump wreckage still being found after 60 years)

Prof. Lu Ren Department of History
Yunnan University 2 North Cuihu
Road Kunming, Yunnan 650091
People's Republic of China Email:
Iuren55@yahoo.com.cn January 6,
2004

Dr. F.B. Evans
4215HardingPike.Apt.708
Nashville, TN 37205
U.S. A

Dear Dr. Evans:

I am Professor Lu Ren, a Vice-director of Department of History, Yunnan University.

We received your letter and enclosed copies (print and computer) of 600 Days in Kunming. It is very wonderful. We appreciate very much your effort in recording your experiences in Kunming in 1944-1945.It is a very good proof of Kunming situation in World War II.

I have very interest in your experiences in Kunming. If you agree, I plan translate your script (600 Days In kunming) in Chinese and publish it in Yunnan University Publishing House so that let more Chinese people know your experiences and the situation of Kunming in W.W. II. So, I need get your letter that you authorize me translate and publish your book (600 Days in Kunming) in Chinese
I look forward to hearing from you soon.

Thank you very much.

With best regards,

[signature]   陆韧

LuRen

ABOUT THE AUTHOR

The book details a part of WWII no one else has written about – how supplies for U.S. forces and the Chinese were handled at the end of the hump air route (Kunming) – the first time a whole country had been supplied by air. Evans treated his entire military service as a learning experience. He listened to all who had interesting stories or experiences to describe.

His memoirs are unusual, personal, and informative. He taped these tales at the urgings of his children to save them for their children and grand-children.

He holds four degrees from the University of Chicago, taught there for 9 years, also at the university of Hawaii (5 years) and at Northwestern (15 years). He published many articles in academic journals and consulted with major automobile, insurance, and brewing companies. He has been listed for years in *Who's Who in America* and *Who's Who in the World*.